EASY BIAS–COVERED
CURVES

Create Quilts with WOW Appeal

WENDY HILL

C&T PUBLISHING

Text © 2006 Wendy Hill

Artwork © 2006 C&T Publishing, Inc.

Publisher: Amy Marson

Editorial Director: Gailen Runge

Acquisitions Editor: Jan Grigsby

Editor: Lynn Koolish

Technical Editors: Ellen Pahl, Susan Nelsen

Copyeditor/Proofreader: Wordfirm Inc.

Cover Designer: Kristen Yenche

Design Director/Book Designer: Kristen Yenche

Illustrator: Richard Sheppard

Production Assistants: Kerry Graham and Kirstie L. Pettersen

Photography: Luke Mulks unless otherwise noted

Additional Photography: Craig Howell and Sharon Risedorph

Published by C&T Publishing, Inc., P.O. Box 1456, Lafayette, CA 94549

Library of Congress Cataloging-in-Publication Data

Hill, Wendy

Easy bias-covered curves : create quilts with wow appeal / Wendy Hill.

     p. cm.

Includes index.

ISBN-13: 978-1-57120-344-1 (paper trade : alk. paper)

ISBN-10: 1-57120-344-3 (paper trade : alk. paper)

1. Patchwork--Patterns. 2. Quilting--Patterns. I. Title.

TT835.H4574 2006

746.46--dc22

                    2006010339

Printed in China

10 9 8 7 6 5 4 3 2 1

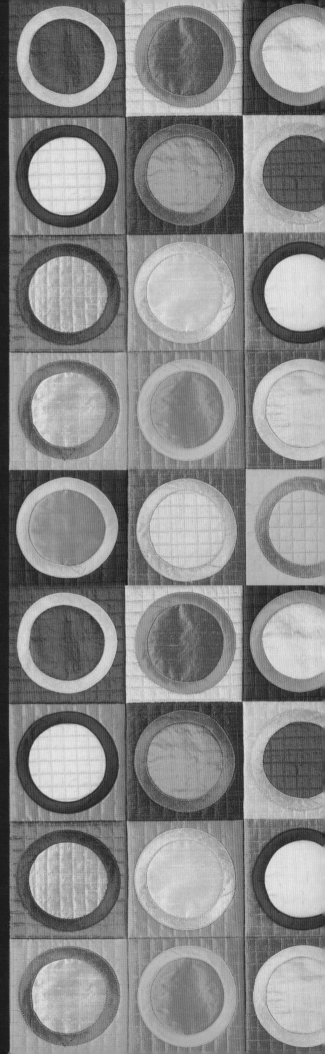

contents

Introduction 6

Get Ready!

Blocks with Curves, Fans, and Wheels 7

Supplies 7

Fabric Selection 8

Fabric Shopping 9

Pressing Matters 9

Get Set!

Templates 11

Cut Out the Fabrics 12

Build the Block 12

Go!

Biased About Bias Tape 14

Cut the Bias Strips 14

Make the Bias Tape 16

Bend the Bias Tape 17

Stitch the Bias Tape 21

Finishing Touches

Borders, Quilting, Binding, Sleeves, and Labels 22

The Block Patterns

Make It Your Own 27

The Adventure Begins 27

Block Pattern 1: Meandering Along 28

Block Pattern 2: Whirling Spirals 38

Block Pattern 3: WhirlyGigging .50

Block Pattern 4: Cutting Corners 58

Block Pattern 5: Making the Rounds 68

Block Pattern 6: Doing Wheelies 80

Resources 93

Meet the Contributors 94

Meet the Author 95

Index 95

DEDICATION

For Quilters Everywhere...

Dream With Your Eyes Open

In Memory of Larraine Scouler

1948–2005

"To live on in the hearts of others is not to die."

Remembering Larraine Scouler

Larraine always began her emails to me with "Olleh Wendy!" How exciting to be able to talk to someone in Australia—literally the other side of the world, where her mornings were my evenings. When I finally asked about the Aussie greeting, I found out it was classic Larraine instead: the down under, back-to-front quilter simply wrote "hello" backward!

Larraine's garden art mimicked her unique approach to life. Among abundant beautiful plants and flowers, Larraine mixed in assorted fun accents, such as broken crockery, a world globe, a dead exercise bike, and a range of blue bottles on poles—all jostling for position with more conventional garden fixtures. In the quilt world she also followed her ideas without categorizing herself as either an art quilter or a traditional quilter, although she went back and forth between those realms with ease. She won prestigious awards; wrote two successful books, *Appliqué Back to Front* (1997, Quilters Resource) and *Quilting Back to Front* (2001, C&T Publishing); volunteered with various quilt-related organizations; and exhibited her work in Australia, Japan, and the United States of America. We all believed she couldn't be stopped, but she lost her battle with leukemia September 20, 2005.

I first met Larraine in the fall of 1997 at International Quilt Market in Houston, Texas. A group of Aussie authors swept through the C&T Publishing booth, carrying me along in their giddy group. Larraine hoped to stand out among all the new authors in Houston, so she had chunks of her naturally red hair dyed magenta. She needn't have worried—her humor, her patch-work genius, and her cheerful, indomitable, and tireless spirit made Larraine stand out in any crowd.

ACKNOWLEDGMENTS

Let me offer a *heartfelt thank-you* to the following people:

- Linda Bussey for squeezing me into her busy machine quilting schedule.

- Mary Buxton, Jane Croley, Susan Howell, Sue McMahan, Joan Metzger, Karla J. Rogers, Kathy Shaker and Carol Webb for saying "yes," not knowing what you were getting into.

- Laura Clark for teaching me her ironing tip "place and press, don't slide and glide," and so much more.

- Sue McMahan for playing hooky at the Bend Film Festival and making labels.

- Karla J. Rogers for listening well and advising wisely.

- Kathy Shaker for letting me "borrow" from the Kathy Shaker Store and being adamant on one of our shopping trips—no more taupe!

- Pen Pals for waiting patiently for the next email.

- Mountain Meadow Quilt Guild for propping me up, helping me out, and making challenge blocks.

- Mrs. Birkenbuel, my high school home economics teacher, for teaching me everything worth knowing about sewing.

- My family for never letting reality get in the way of imagination!

Thank you to the following companies who generously supported the making of this book:

Quilter's Dream Batting

Sulky of America

Timeless Treasures

ANYTHING GOES Wendy Hill, with blocks made by Judi Brown, Christine Hindle Drumright, Pauly Ruth Edwards, Sheila Finzer, Janet Gehlert, Susan Howell, Sarah Kaufman, Beverly King, Crys Kyle, Joan Metzger, Janice Mottau, Dolores Petty, Karla J. Rogers, Linda Saukkonen, and BJ Tinker, 63¾″ × 63¾″; quilted by Linda Bussey

In response to my block challenge, 15 people made 73 blocks with a scrappy color scheme. Sixty of the blocks ended up in the quilt, with the blocks on point.

INTRODUCTION

Lucky us! We quilters get to live in our imagination, connected to a network of other quilters. Playing with color, texture, and pattern, we create beautiful quilts to give as gifts, to offer as comfort in a crisis, to display as art, or to wrap love around our family members and friends—all just for the pure enjoyment and satisfaction of it. With our hands, heart, and mind, and just a *few* supplies, we make quilts!

My imagination led me to thinking about circles. I found circles everywhere around me, in fabrics, architecture, nature, and even in the patterns of car rims. Nonquilters told me I was obsessed, but I know you understand—I just wanted to make quilts with circles, curves, arcs, and wavy lines.

So I did. After finishing a wallhanging with 256 *pieced* curved seams, I decided to experiment with *covered* curves. Pieced curves are great, but covering the curves allows beginners to try out patterns too daunting to piece and gives quilters of all levels an opportunity to play with design. There is a place for piecing curved seams, but not in this book.

Look at two quilts with the same basic pattern. The first quilt *shows* pieced curves; the second quilt *shows off* covered curves. The bias-covered seams add another design element to the pattern, a bonus that adds complexity without adding difficulty.

Detail of *In the Woods*, Wendy Hill; **covered** curves

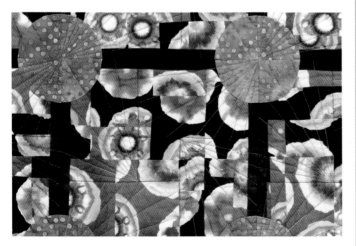

Detail of *Circling the Block*, Wendy Hill; **pieced** curves

Please join me on my island of imagination. The next three chapters introduce the basics of curvy patterns, including my method of building blocks (instead of piecing) and making bias tape to cover the curves. Each of the six block pattern chapters provides a small project to start you off plus plenty of ideas, samples, and tips for making your own version. Be sure to look for the challenge quilt in each chapter, made by someone just like you. Each person took my block pattern idea and ran with it—and so can you. But wait, there's more: Each chapter concludes with even more ideas for making quilts with related curvy block patterns.

Experiment with individual blocks as you learn this new technique. Even simple techniques like this one take a little practice, so don't put pressure on yourself to make a masterpiece the first time around. To each project, simply bring your creative spirit and your desire to make quilts. Let this book guide you through the process of making your own quilts with WOW appeal. Come on, let's go sew!

GeT ReaDY!

Blocks with Curves, Fans, and Wheels

Look at blocks with curves, fans, and wheels with a new confidence and sense of excitement. Almost all of these blocks can be adapted to covering the curves instead of carefully piecing them. Once you understand the process, there will be nothing to stop you.

Quilts with covered curves follow the same basic assembly process as pieced quilts: units go together to make blocks, and blocks go together to make a quilt top. The big difference is the curves. The curves are covered, eliminating the need to piece curved seams.

Covering the curves rather than piecing them has an added benefit: The covered curves add another design element—bands of color and texture—to the pattern. It's so easy, anyone can achieve success.

Supplies

General supplies

Bias maker: This is a handy gadget used to make your own bias tape. Bias tape makers come in several widths, from ¼″ to 2″. Look for the kind that have a colored plastic insert in the middle, which grip the fabric better than all-metal bias makers. For the projects in this book, you'll need bias makers in ¼″, ⅜″, ½″, and ¾″ sizes. Bias makers are available in quilt shops, fabric stores, and by mail order.

Measuring tape: You'll need a flexible measuring tape to measure curved edges.

Mechanical pencil: The consistently sharp point of a mechanical pencil is more accurate than the tip of a regular pencil, which quickly becomes dull.

Paper: Use freezer paper to make templates; use newsprint or graph paper to draw your own patterns.

Rotary cutter and cutting mat: Use a rotary cutter and mat for cutting bias strips and other parts of your quilt.

Rotary cutting ruler: I use the 6″ × 24″ ruler most of the time when cutting bias strips. The ruler needs to have the 45° angle line printed on it.

Silk pins: These wonderful pins are very fine and allow you to pin fabric pieces without warps and wobbles.

Spray water bottle: I always keep a water bottle by my ironing board. It comes in handy when pressing fabric before cutting and again after stitching the bias curves. Lightly mist water onto the fabric, then press with the iron. You'll love the results.

Sulky Soft 'n Sheer: This extremely lightweight but durable nonwoven textured nylon stabilizer is used as a foundation for block assembly. You can substitute a different lightweight nonwoven interfacing or woven fabric.

Tailor's clapper: This smooth piece of hardwood is used in pressing. The clapper holds in the heat and steam of the iron without harming the fabric. See page 10 for easy directions to make your own.

Walking foot: This foot helps feed the layers of fabric through the feed dogs evenly. It works well when zigzagging curves and topstitching the bias tape.

Fabric Selection

Colors talk. Colors don't say much by themselves, but put them together, and you'll hear a racket. Take a pile of fabrics, and listen to the visual conversation. Observe what happens when colors collide. Rearrange the pile, add fabrics, delete fabrics—observe how the conversation changes. Colors talk to each other, but more important is the conversation colors have with you. This is what I call color sensibility—something all of us can develop with experience and *without* formal color theory.

Evaluate color choices with a group of fabrics placed side by side, because that is how you'll see fabrics in a finished quilt. Quickly assemble a pile of fabric bolts, or cut pieces without laboring over individual choices. Observe the stack of fabrics from all angles and distances. Delete or add to the stack of fabrics. How does the color conversation change? This process of brainstorming fabric choices allows you to sidestep your usual preferences and prejudices. You'll end up with an interesting group of fabrics, and you'll develop your color sensibility.

The color, value, texture, and size of prints all go into the decision-making process when choosing fabric for any quilt project. With bias-covered curves, the self-made bias tape adds another design element to the block pattern—another excuse to acquire and use more fabric. See page 37 for more on selecting fabric.

◎ FABRIC FOR BIAS TAPE

The fabric used for the bias tape should be visible when the block is finished, but the visibility can range from low to high contrast with the other fabrics. Stripes, checks, plaids, and small prints usually contrast well, just because of their visual texture, but medium and large prints can also work. Experiment with a variety of choices to find the fabric that adds to the overall design of your quilt.

Start by auditioning fabric at home or at the fabric store. Fold the fabric at a 45° angle. Place a piece of paper parallel to the fold, leaving a narrow band exposed. If the fabric design is lost on the bias or just doesn't look right, the fabric is unsuitable.

Visualize bias tape without cutting fabric.

Move the likely fabrics on to the next step. Sandwich the folded fabric between pieces or bolts of the other fabrics. Stand back, and see how it looks. With your own fabric, cut sample strips the finished size of the bias tape across the corner of the piece of fabric. Audition the strips with the other fabrics or on partially finished, zigzagged blocks to see how they look. The bias tape should add to the design. If the bias tape disappears, leaves you with a flat feeling, or dominates the quilt, it's probably not suitable.

Experiment with simple cut strips first.

Look through the photographs of quilts and block samples in the book to get an idea of the variety of fabric that works for bias tape. Some quilts use one fabric for all of the bias; other quilts use several. Here are a few examples that show the range of possibilities.

Detail of *Cool, Clear Water*, Jane C. Croley; one multicolor batik for all bias tape (see complete quilt on page 29)

Detail of *Around and About*, Wendy Hill; solid colors are perfect here (see complete quilt on page 68)

Detail of *Girlie Girl*, Wendy Hill; three bias fabrics work here—print, stripe, and check (see complete quilt on page 58)

Detail of *Anything Goes*, Wendy Hill; each block has different bias tape (see complete quilt on page 5)

Fabric Shopping

Each of the six block patterns includes a small project to get you started, complete with a supply list and step-by-step directions. For those who decide to adjust the directions to make their own project, here are some hints for estimating fabric yardage.

If estimating yardage is new to you, don't panic. First, look over the project supply list. You'll be able to make a good guess about how much fabric you'll need with this information. Or make a good educated guess by estimating how many pattern pieces could be cut from a quarter yard of fabric. Use this number to figure out how many quarter yards you'll need altogether. Another idea is to use a lot of fabrics, twenty or more, for a scrappy look. No one will ever know if you substitute a new fabric after running out. Finally, do what quilters everywhere do: buy fabric in one of two amounts— a lot and a lot more!

With experience, you'll get a feel for how much fabric is needed for the bias tape. Until then, see Estimating Yardage for Bias Tape on page 15.

Pressing Matters

I press seams open—most of the time. The resulting flat, smooth quilt top is easier to hand or machine quilt. Instead of following a hard-and-fast rule about pressing, press seams open or to one side depending on the situation.

◎ TO STEAM OR NOT TO STEAM

It's not the steam that distorts fabric, it's the sliding, gliding, and scrubbing with the iron. Remember this chant while ironing: "place and press; don't slide and glide." Whether you use steam or not, and I usually do, always lift the iron up and down while pressing for best results.

◎ TAILOR'S CLAPPER

This hardwood tool for pressing comes from the tailoring industry, but it also works well for making quilts. I use a clapper in all (or almost all) of my sewing and pressing of quilts, clothing, and so on. A clapper really flattens the fabric and makes the pressed item look crisp and fantastic, and the fabric stays "pressed" longer. If you hold an iron down on the fabric, the heat and/or steam continues to build up and it doesn't take long for the fabric to scorch. By holding the heat and steam to the fabric with the clapper, you get the effect of the iron without the scorching. In general, heavier irons give better pressing results, but if you have a lightweight iron and a clapper, you'll get even better results.

Hold the iron in one hand and the clapper in the other. Place and press with the iron, then trap the heat (and steam) with the clapper. Try it—you'll love the results!

MAKE YOUR OWN CLAPPER
All you need is a piece of hardwood, approximately 3″ × 8″ × 1¾″. Sand the edges smooth, and you're ready to press!
tiP

Now that you've looked at curved blocks in a new way, they won't seem so intimidating. Read on to learn how to make blocks with covered curves.

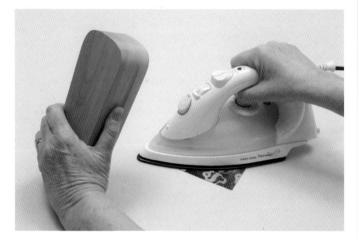

Place and press.

Hold in heat (and steam) with clapper—no scorching!

Sewing together the units of a block with covered curves is similar to constructing a pieced block. The big difference is that the curves are covered, not pieced; there are no curved seams and no seam allowances along the curved edges. However, the blocks or units are still sewn right sides together, so all straight edges must always include a seam allowance.

Templates

Freezer-paper templates are easy to make and use. The freezer paper temporarily sticks to the fabric until the shape is cut out. You can peel off the freezer paper and reuse it, but multiple templates of the same shape speed up the cutting process.

The simplest patterns have no internal straight seams in the block. You can draw the pattern right on the paper side of the freezer paper, adding your seam allowance around the straight sides. Cut out the block, and then cut it apart along the curved lines. You now have templates.

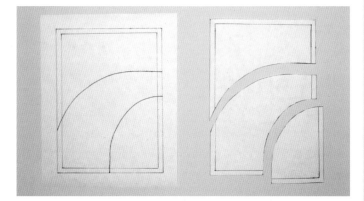

Cut apart along curved lines.

For block patterns with internal straight seams where units join together to make the block, trace or draw the pattern on graph paper or newsprint first.

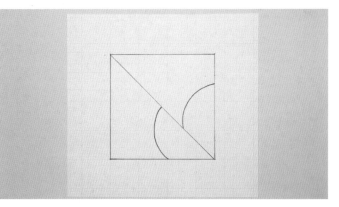

Trace or draw pattern on graph paper.

Cut apart the units along the straight sides. Glue the pieces onto freezer paper, leaving room to add the seam allowance on each pattern piece along the straight sides.

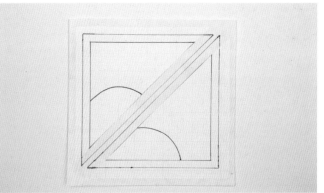

Add seam allowances on straight sides.

Cut out the pieces along the straight and curved lines.

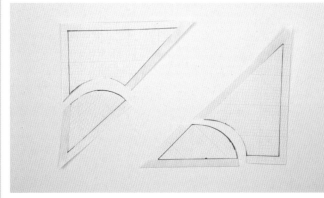

Templates are ready to use.

Seam Allowances

The standard seam allowance for quilting is $\frac{1}{4}$", no more and no less. This rule is passed down from book to book, quilter to quilter, and teacher to student. I escaped inheriting this rule by being self-taught in the days before there were books and teachers to tell me otherwise.

I use a wider seam allowance—up to a full $\frac{3}{8}$" wide. I line up the side of my regular foot with the fabric. I move the needle over to make the seam as wide as I want it, using the needle position feature found on most sewing machines. This is why I still use a wider seam allowance today:

- The regular presser foot is larger than a $\frac{1}{4}$" foot. The regular foot really grips the fabric, giving me more control as I sew.

- The wider seam allowance is more forgiving. If I need to fudge a skimpy edge, there is room with the wider seam allowance to do it.

- It is easier to press seams open with wider seam allowances. When seams are pressed open, the whole quilt top is flatter, smoother, and easier to quilt.

I don't expect you to use wider seam allowances just because I recommend it. But try it out for yourself, and you might be surprised at the results.

Cut Out the Fabrics

Place the waxy side of the freezer-paper template down on the right side of the fabric. It's okay to cluster the templates together without regard to the grain line of the fabric because you will use a foundation to keep the unit or block from stretching. Lightly press the templates with a warm iron to make them temporarily stick in place.

Cut out the fabric shapes with scissors or a rotary cutter. Avoid shaving off slivers of the paper template. Make a habit of cutting the *outside* curves about $\frac{1}{8}$" away from the edge of the template. Cut all *inside* curves right along the edge of the template. This prevents gapping later.

Cut *outside* curves about $\frac{1}{8}$" from edge of template; cut *inside* curves along edge of template.

Remove the freezer paper by peeling the paper off the fabric, not the other way around. That will prevent any stretching or distortion of the fabric.

Build the Block

Since we are not piecing the curved seams of the block, think of this process as *building* the block, instead of piecing it. And because there are no seams along the curves, the fabric needs support under the covered curves, so you will build the block on a permanent foundation material, such as Sulky Soft 'n Sheer. I really like this product because it is extremely light-weight, but durable and soft. It does not need to be torn away and is left in the quilt. It will not affect the drape or softness of your quilt in any way. You can use other foundation materials, but Sulky Soft 'n Sheer is my favorite.

1. Cut the permanent foundation material the same size as the unit or block, *including* the seam allowances on the straight sides.

2. Place the cut fabric shapes onto the foundation, overlapping the inner curve over the outer curve. Remember, the inner curve is cut right along the edge of the template, so it accurately represents the seamline. Pin the pieces in place all around; place pins perpendicular to any areas that will be stitched.

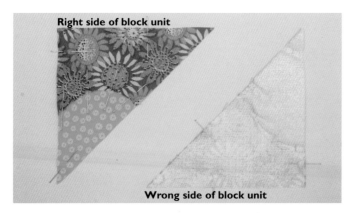

Place cut fabric shapes onto foundation. Pin.

3. Adjust your machine for a narrow but open zigzag stitch. The width setting should put the zig and the zag just over the raw edges. The stitch length should be long enough so that you can see through the zigzags but not so far apart that the fabric leaps through the feed dogs. Zigzag the raw edges of curves through all the layers, removing pins as you sew. Use a walking foot to guarantee even feeding of the fabric.

Zigzag raw edges of curves.

tip Zigzagging, the miracle stitch, eases and secures the raw edges in place. You might be tempted to skip this step, but I encourage you to learn from the mistakes of those who have gone before you: *always* zigzag the raw edges. Without zigzagging, fabrics buckle around the bias tape, or worse, raw edges pull out from under the stitched bias tape. This step pays for itself with carefree sewing later and flawless results.

Background As Foundation

Some block patterns lend themselves to using the background fabric as the foundation. Cut the background fabric the same size as the finished unit or block, *including* the seam allowance. Because this piece is the foundation, it must be cut along the grain line of the fabric. Cut the curved pattern piece out along the edge of the template (without adding $\frac{1}{8}''$ to the outer curve). Place the curved pattern piece onto the background fabric, and pin; zigzag the curved edge.

Note: After stitching the bias tape in place, you may want to cut away the excess fabric from the back, especially if the top fabric is see-through.

Background fabric is foundation.   Zigzag curves.

The next chapter tells all about the magic of self-made bias tape and how to use it. After doing a test sample of a finished block, assemble a large group of blocks before continuing to the next step. Working on the same step with a group of blocks allows the brain to get into a groove or rhythm; you'll be more efficient and less likely to make mistakes.

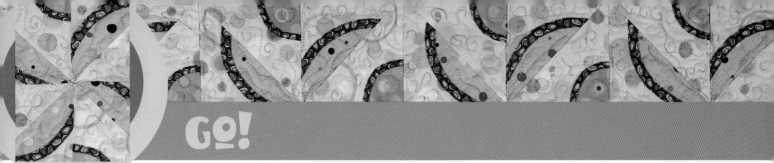

Biased About Bias Tape

I love the way bias tape appears to be painstakingly pieced inserts of fabric instead of a topstitched seam covering. It does take some time to create the bias tape, pin it in place, and stitch it down, but quilters at just about any level can experience instant success using this method. Purchased bias tape may be used, but it's more fun to choose your own fabrics and make your own.

Cut the Bias Strips

No matter which method you use to make the bias tape, all of the methods start with strips of fabric cut along the true bias of the fabric. The true bias is found at a 45° angle to the lengthwise and crosswise grain of the fabric.

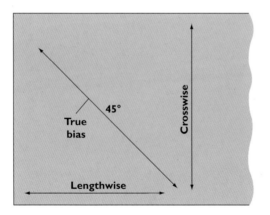

Find true bias.

1. Open up the fabric, and work with a single layer. Use a rotary cutting ruler with a 45° line printed on it. Line up the 45° line on the ruler with the lengthwise grain of the fabric (selvage). Make the first cut.

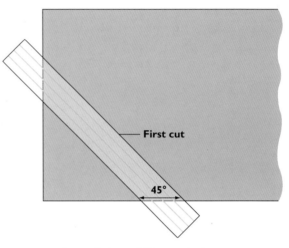

Cut single layer of fabric; make first cut.

2. Cut strips twice as wide as the width of the finished bias tape. For example, if the finished width of the bias tape is ½″, cut the strip 1″ wide. Cut as many strips as needed. After 6 to 8 cuts, reposition the ruler to check the 45° angle—cut a new edge if necessary. That ensures the accuracy of the 45° angle.

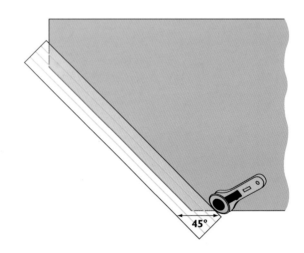

Cut width twice as wide as finished bias tape.

tip It can be pesky to make narrow ¼″ bias strips. If the ½″ cut strip flattens out instead of folding correctly or otherwise misbehaves, cut the strip ⁹⁄₁₆″ instead. This is halfway between ½″ and ⅝″.

Estimating Yardage for Bias Tape

A handy reference chart is provided below to help you determine how much bias tape you can cut from a given amount of fabric. This will help you estimate how much fabric you need to buy. The numbers in the chart are based on fabric that is 40″ wide; the calculations do not include the corners of the yardage.

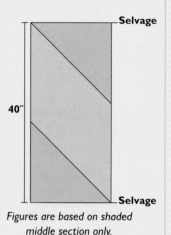

Figures are based on shaded middle section only.

You'll need to estimate the total number of pieces of bias tape you'll need, and how long they should be. To do this, follow these steps:

1. Measure the curve by placing your measuring tape on end so it will bend around the curve. Add an extra inch for leeway.

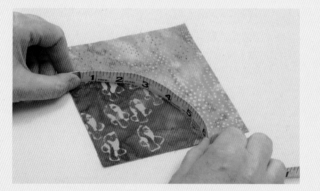

Measuring tape on edge bends with curve.

2. Decide how wide the finished bias tape should be. Your strips will be cut twice as wide as the desired finished width.

3. Count the total number of pieces of each length you'll need for all the blocks.

4. Use this information and the chart provided to determine how much fabric you'll need.

Once you see how much fabric you need, it's a good idea to round up and buy a little extra, especially when you are first trying the technique. As an example, let's say the curve measures 7″; with the extra 1″, it becomes 8″. The bias will finish at ½″ wide, and there are 20 blocks. You'll need 20 pieces cut 8″ long. Look at the chart. Find the column for ½″ finished bias tape, and look down the chart. A ¼ yard of fabric isn't enough; there are only 19 strips 12″ long. Move to ⅜ yard. That will give you plenty because you can cut 17 strips 19″ long from the fabric (you can cut two 8″ lengths from each strip).

Number of Bias Strips Cut From Common Yardages

Fabric Quantity	Finished Width of Bias Tape			
	¼″	⅜″	½″	¾″
¼ yard	39 strips, ½″ × 12″	26 strips, ¾″ × 12″	19 strips, 1″ × 12″	13 strips, 1½″ × 12″
⅜ yard	35 strips, ½″ × 19″	24 strips, ¾″ × 19″	17 strips, 1″ × 19″	12 strips, 1½″ × 19″
½ yard	30 strips, ½″ × 24″	20 strips, ¾″ × 24″	12 strips, 1″ × 24″	10 strips, 1½″ × 24″

Make the Bias Tape

Make bias tape with purchased bias makers as I do, or use the method you prefer. As with other techniques in quilting, we each develop our own favorites.

◎ PURCHASED BIAS MAKERS

Purchased bias makers come in a variety of sizes starting as narrow as ¼". Commonly used sizes for covering curves are ¼", ⅜", ½", and ¾" wide. Read the directions that come with the bias maker before following these directions.

1. Cut the strip of fabric for the width of bias you need (twice as wide the desired finished width). The end of the strip should be cleanly cut at an angle so that it will feed through the bias maker more easily.

Cut end of strip at angle.

2. Insert the bias strip into the bias maker. If you are right-handed, pin one end of the fabric strip to the right end of the ironing board. Hold the bias maker in your left hand and start to pull the bias maker away from the pin. The edges of the fabric strip fold to the middle.

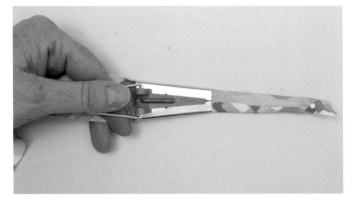

Pull bias maker away from pin.

3. Set the iron to a steam setting. Press the newly folded strip with the iron as it emerges from the bias maker.

Place iron; press.

 tip If the steam of the iron burns your fingers, turn off the steam and mist the ironing board cover with water instead. By making the bias tape over the lightly dampened ironing board cover, you get the effect of steam without blasting your fingers.

 tip If the cut strip is not long enough, join the strips with a diagonal seam before making the bias tape. Baste the seam open by hand with a running stitch. This trick allows the pieced strip to flow smoothly through the bias maker.

4. Wrap the finished bias tape around a piece of cardboard, and pin the end to itself. Some fabrics hold a crease better than others, but all finished bias tape is capable of popping open if left alone long enough.

Wrap finished bias tape around cardboard.

◎ HAND-FOLDING METHOD

You can also make any width of bias tape with the following method.

1. Cut the strip of fabric on a true bias twice as wide as the desired finished width.

2. Place the cut strip of fabric right side down on the ironing board.

3. Fold one side to the middle, and press until one side is finished.

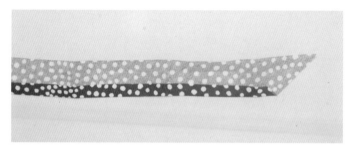

Fold first side; press.

4. Repeat with the other side.

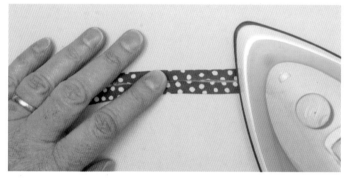

Fold second side; press.

5. Wrap the bias tape around cardboard, and pin.

Bend the Bias Tape

The magic of using bias tape occurs at this step. By using a few pins, misting with water, and pressing with a steam setting, you can bend the bias and it will conform to the curve. The bias bends easier on shallow curves, but it will also bend on tighter curves with a few more pins. It may feel awkward to place and pin the bias tape, but just keep at it. Soon it will be second nature to you.

◎ ARCS AND PARTIAL CIRCLES

Note that in the photos below, the outer curve is already covered with bias, whereas the inner curve is shown in progress. This is to show how the bias tape looks after it is stitched, as compared with what it looks like before stitching when it is pinned.

1. Place the block on your work surface so the inside of the curve is closest to you and at the bottom of the block. Place the bias tape on edge along the curve, letting both ends extend about ½″. Trim off the extra length.

Trim bias tape.

2. Start in the middle of the curve. Center the bias tape over the curve, and pin perpendicular to the bias tape.

Pin perpendicular to bias tape.

3. Start in the middle of the bias tape. Work your fingers along the curve, pinning as you move to the edge of the fabric. Make sure the bias tape is centered over the curve all the way to the edge of the fabric. Repeat this process from the middle to the other side.

Pin as you position bias tape.

4. Lightly mist the bias tape with water. With the pins still in place, gently press with the iron set on steam. Now is the time to use a clapper (see pages 9–10). The bias tape bends into the curve, almost like magic.

Press lightly with iron.

Bias tape conforms to curve.

⊚ WHOLE CIRCLES

It's easy to cover the curve of whole circles with a continuous loop of bias tape. Follow the steps below to see how it's done. (**Note:** The block is shown ready to go with a zigzagged circle on a background fabric.)

1. To measure the circumference (the outside edge) of the circle, mark a starting point with a pin. Place the measuring tape on edge, and measure all the way around the circle, beginning and ending at the pin. Be sure to keep the measuring tape on the curve while measuring. Repeat the process to make sure you get the same measurement a second time.

Measure circumference.

2. Add the *cut width* of the bias strip to the circumference. This will give you the total length needed. For example, if the circumference of the circle is 25˝ and the cut width of the bias tape is 1˝, then the total length required is 26˝. Make a length of bias tape a few inches longer than that.

3. Cut the finished bias strip to this exact figure, using a rotary cutting ruler to cut both ends at right angles.

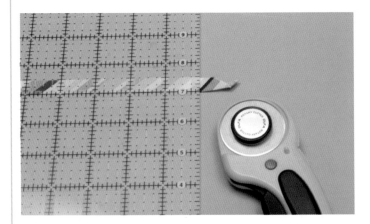

Use rotary cutting ruler to cut ends at right angles.

4. To join the ends right sides together using a diagonal seam, make sure the strip is not twisted. Open up the folds, line up the ends perpendicular to each other with right sides together, and pin. Mark the diagonal sewing line from the top corner to the corner underneath with a ruler and your favorite marking tool. Make sure the ruler is aligned from corner to corner.

Match ends; mark sewing line.

5. Sew on the line, backstitching at the start and finish. Check to make sure both ends line up at the seam. **Note:** If the fold lines don't match, it's okay.

Bias seam

Place a piece of tissue paper under the seam when sewing the ends of bias tape together. This stabilizes the fabric and makes it easier to sew straight. Fold and tear off the tissue paper before continuing.

6. Trim off the excess, leaving a ¼″ seam allowance. Press the seam open. Refold the bias tape, and press. The continuous loop of bias tape is ready to use. It might not look as if it will bend around a circle and lie flat, but it will.

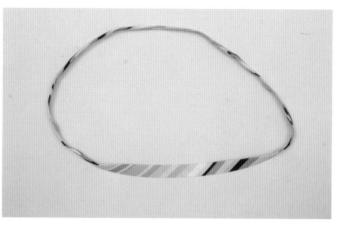

Finished continuous loop of bias tape

7. Fold the loop in half. Place a pin at both folds. Refold the loop in half again, lining up the 2 pins. Place a pin at both folds. Now the loop is divided into equal fourths.

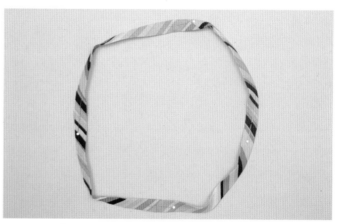

Pins mark equal fourths.

8. Fold the paper template made for the original circle into fourths. Use the fold lines to mark the quarter points on the fabric with pins.

Use paper template to divide fabric circle into fourths.

9. Remove the paper template. Pin the bias tape to the circle, matching up the pins on both. Always pin with the point inserted into the inner edge of the bias tape.

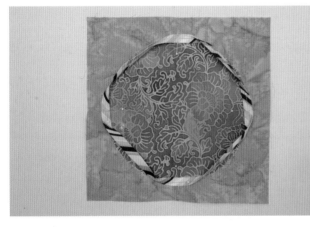

Match pins.

Insert pin at inner edge of bias.

10. Work your fingers around the curve, placing and pinning the bias tape as you move to the next pin. Adjust the bias tape as needed to bend it into a smooth circle. Use a total of 8 to 16 pins. Expect the bias tape to roll a bit between pins.

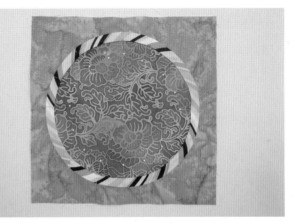

Use 8 to 16 pins.

11. Set the iron to a steam setting. Lightly mist the bias tape with water. Hold the iron lightly over the bias tape. This is a good time to use a clapper (see pages 9-10).

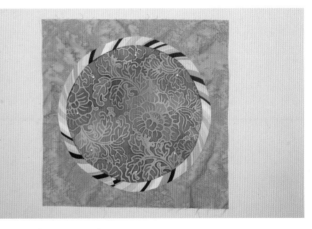

Bias tape conforms to circle.

SMALL CIRCLES

Making a continuous bias loop conform to a small circle is just as easy, but there is a trick: Make the bias loop conform to the circle on paper first. If it pleats or crunches, it's okay, because this is a dress rehearsal for the bias loop. After this treatment, the bias loop will easily conform to the fabric circle.

I. Draw the same size circle onto blank typing paper. Mark the quarter points on both the bias tape and the paper circle. Match up the quarter points and pin, using about 8 pins. Mist with water, and press. The loop might crumple, pleat, or otherwise look impossible. Just allow it to sit until it's almost or completely dry.

Dress rehearsal on paper for bias loop

2. Remove the bias loop from the paper. Place the loop on the ironing board, right side up. Cover with a press cloth or piece of muslin, and then smooth flat. Lightly mist the muslin, and press. Like magic, the bias loop will ease into a flat circle. Use the bias loop to cover the curves of the fabric circle.

Smooth, flat bias loop ready to use

Stitch the Bias Tape

Always stitch the inside curve first using a thread color that matches the bias tape fabric. Remove the pins as you sew. Then stitch the outside curve. For partial curves, backstitch at both ends of the stitching line. For whole circles, tug on the bobbin thread to pull the top thread to the back, and tie off.

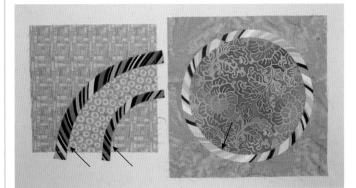

Stitch inside curve first.

◎ TOPSTITCHING TIPS

1. Use a fresh, sharp needle, such as a Schmetz Microtex Sharp, in a size to match your thread.

2. Use a walking foot. It will walk around curves quite easily.

3. Use a single-hole throat plate if you have one. That enhances the stitch quality without any extra effort.

4. Start and end partial seams with backstitching. For whole circles, pull the threads to the back, and tie off.

5. Stop with the needle down. Move the needle to the up position before starting to stitch again. This prevents that crooked first stitch when sewing resumes.

6. Sew slowly and steadily, with no radical movements. If you get an itch, stop sewing. If the cat jumps on the table, stop sewing. If there is housework, keep on sewing!

Now you're almost ready to start your own covered-curve quilting adventure! Make one of the Get Started Projects starting on page 31, or strike out on your own.

Borders, Quilting, Binding, Sleeves, and Labels

If you need more help than is provided in this book with quilting basics, such as borders, quilting, binding, sleeves, and labels, please consult a reference book (see Resources, on page 93, for some good basic quilting books), a friend, or your local friendly fabric store clerks, who will be happy to assist you.

◉ BORDERS

If the quilt shown doesn't have a border, you always have the option of adding one yourself. Look over the following examples for ideas that go beyond a basic frame type of border.

A simple frame border, as in the following two quilts, can pack a lot of "wow" power.

Detail of *Windmills*, Susan Howell; two narrow borders plus binding look like one border (see complete quilt on page 56)

Detail of *In the Woods*, Wendy Hill; mitered corners with striped fabric (see complete quilt on page 59)

Extend the pattern into the border to add an extra finishing touch to the quilt.

Detail of *Really Red*, Wendy Hill and Kathy H. Shaker; extra round of rectangles and corner squares acts as border (see complete quilt on page 60)

Detail of *Fabricated Enigma*, Joan Metzger; same block cut on diagonal fits together for border (see complete quilt on page 29)

Use leftover fabrics to create a pieced border.

Detail of *Girlie Girl*, Wendy Hill; carry string piecing into border (see complete quilt on page 58)

Detail of *Rings*, Wendy Hill; random piecing makes great border (see complete quilt on page 69)

◉ QUILTING

The focus of this book is on covered curve patterns, so the project directions tell you to quilt your project as desired. Although I am comfortable with free-motion quilting, I used my trusty walking foot and beautiful variegated thread for most of these quilts. Simple straight-line quilting can be a nice contrast to the curves of the fabric. Look over these close-ups for ideas of your own.

Simple grid quilting can be very effective by incorporating high-contrast thread or wavy lines. I always look for shortcuts, so I mark the first line with masking tape and then use the edge of my presser foot as a guide whenever possible.

Detail of *Rim Runner*, Wendy Hill; variegated thread enhances straight line grid (see complete quilt on page 81)

Detail of *Around and About*, Wendy Hill; quilting each block first made grids easy to do (see complete quilt on page 68)

Use a straight stitch with the walking foot to echo the block pattern or a curve. It looks like free-motion quilting, but it's not—even beginner machine quilters can do this.

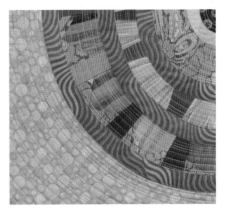

Detail of *Rings*, Wendy Hill; quilting lines echo fabric rings (see complete quilt on page 69)

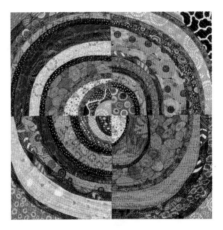

Detail of *Roads Not Taken*, Wendy Hill; closely spaced quilting lines echo design (see complete quilt on page 28)

Detail of *Tivoli Garden*, Wendy Hill; surface stitched wavy lines echo pattern of background fabric (see complete quilt on page 80)

Many sewing machines have a built-in stitch for a wavy line. By altering the default setting, the wavy line can be almost straight or quite curvy. Use this stitch alone or in combination with straight lines for very effective and fun results.

It's possible to quilt individual blocks to the batting first, and then assemble the blocks together into a quilt top. Layer the quilted top with the backing fabric, and add a bit more quilting, usually by stitching in the ditch. It's easier to handle the quilt in smaller sections, plus *stops and starts* of quilting lines are no problem. Clean out the bobbin area frequently because of the extra lint.

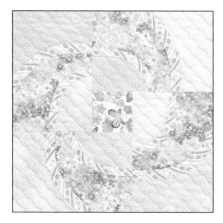

Detail of *Butterfly Breeze*, Wendy Hill; parallel wavy lines on diagonal add breeziness (see complete quilt on page 39)

Detail of *Tokyo Twist*, Wendy Hill; wavy lines alternate with straight stitching to accent twist (see complete quilt on page 38)

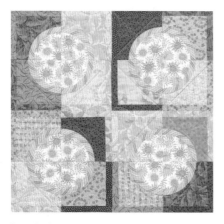

Detail of *In the Woods*, Wendy Hill; wavy lines alternate with straight stitching in a grid (see complete quilt on page 59)

Detail of *Razzle Dazzle*, Wendy Hill; complex quilting designs are easier when completed in sections first (see complete quilt on page 91)

Detail of *Somewhere...*, Joan Metzger; quilting each block let Joan easily stitch rays (see complete quilt on page 48)

◎ BINDING

The binding finishes the outer edge of the quilt. I think about design all the way to the outer edge of my quilts and consider binding an integral part of the design. There are a lot of options. Follow your own preferences for single- or double-fold binding, fabric cut on the bias or the straight of the grain, and hand or machine stitching the edge. You can also include filled or unfilled piping around the inside edge of the binding. Piping brings out colors and makes the fabric medley sing. Remember when auditioning fabrics that the binding will be a narrow band against all the other fabrics.

I use a wider binding that finishes between ⅜″ and ½″ because I like it to be seen, especially on a larger quilt. I stitch with a ⅜″ seam so that the binding is nicely filled by the batting after folding it to the back.

Detail of *Rings*, Wendy Hill; binding fabric blends into design of quilt top instead of framing quilt, allowing design to go right to edge (see complete quilt on page 69)

Detail of *Drop in the Bucket*, Wendy Hill and Jane Crowley; binding is made up of pieced-together fabrics from arcs, to carry on feeling of water; binding with just one fabric would have made hard edge around quilt; this way it flows (see complete quilt on page 31)

Detail of *Girlie Girl*, Wendy Hill; example of striped fabric used for binding, with stripes running perpendicular to quilt; hot pink and metallic stripes stand up to quilt and hold their own when cut this way (see complete quilt on page 58)

Detail of *In the Woods*, Wendy Hill; narrow inner border and binding are same fabric; repeating fabric helps define quilt in interesting way by making border a unit of inner border, stripe, and binding; it doesn't just frame quilt, it makes whole surface design cohesive (see complete quilt on page 59)

Detail of *Razzle Dazzle*, Wendy Hill; striped fabric is cut on bias and picks up and accents colors used in quilt top; there is nice interplay of binding with quilt top (see complete quilt on page 91)

You can also consider using a facing instead of a binding. This option is especially useful for wall quilts when the impact of the design is hampered by a hard edge surrounding the quilt.

Whirlygigs, Carol Loehndorf-Webb; pinwheels seem capable of spinning right off edge (see complete quilt on page 51)

Whirlygigs; detail of facing on back of quilt

SLEEVES

Hang your quilts easily and professionally with a hemmed sleeve or casing sewn to the back of the quilt. The sleeve should finish at about 4″ wide and be 2″ less than the width of the quilt. Prepare a slat of acrylic or wood with 2 holes in the upper top corners for hanging. Slide the slat through the sleeve. Hang the board with small picture nails. From the front, the quilt sits flat and snug against the wall.

tip Some quilters use a board or slat at the bottom of the quilt as well to add weight and help keep the quilt snug to the wall. Prepare a sleeve in the same manner as described above, and attach it along the bottom of the quilt. **Note:** A bottom board will not cure warped, wavy quilts.

LABELS

Always add a label to the back of your quilt. Include basic information such as the quilt title, your name and state, and the date. Use photo transfers and printing on fabric to add the type of information that you wish you knew about antique quilts. Include cleaning instructions for quilts you give away. Use a permanent pen, hand embroidery, printing on fabric, or machine-stitched lettering to create your label.

THE BLOCK PATTERNS

Make It Your Own

When you decide to make a project from a book or magazine, you probably already use the Make It Your Own concept. You adjust the directions, substitute your own color choices, change the layout, and so on to satisfy your own creative streak. The next six block pattern chapters are geared toward taking an idea and running with it—making the patterns your own.

It's all about imagination. Let me tell you about the time I found a stack of steeply discounted plates at a kitchen outlet shop. The salesperson overheard me telling my friend how I could use the plates to serve appetizers. She interrupted us to explain patiently that I could not use the stack of saucers as serving plates, because after all, they were saucers. Even though the matching cups were long gone (hence the great sale price), they were still saucers, not plates. It was obvious, she said. Fortunately, you and I and other quilters have plenty of imagination. We can see beyond *what is* to *what could be* with saucers as well as fabrics.

Each block pattern chapter shows the pattern used in three quilts and three individual blocks. That's six color combinations and *looks* per chapter. Look for the challenge quilt in each chapter, made by a quilter much like you. The women who accepted the challenge took my pattern ideas and made them their own, just like you can. Use the Get Started Project, with complete directions from start to finish, to make a quilt like the sample or to make your own version. Whether you adjust the pattern a little or a lot, your own quilt will be unique.

The Adventure Begins

You already have what you need to create your own projects: a love of color and texture, and a desire to make quilts. Take the time you need, and enjoy the process. Soon enough you'll have a wonderful finished quilt and a zillion more ideas for the next project!

Meandering Along

 A circle obsession led to this mix of more than 50 different textured fabrics. I drew 9 different big blocks to get the 36 individual blocks needed for this layout. Even the bias fabrics are dotty!

ROADS NOT TAKEN Wendy Hill, 56″ × 56″

Get to Know the Block

Many traditional blocks use arcs to create the pattern. My variation, Meandering Along, uses freehand, imperfect arcs. The options for layout are almost endless, ranging from symmetrical patterns like Barn Raising, Straight Furrows, and whole circles, to totally random arrangements. Either way, the lines of the arcs will not line up—that is intentional. This pattern is fun and easy to make, with no curved seams, no perfection required, and *WOW!* design impact.

This is a good pattern to use with a lot of different fabrics. Select the fabrics around a color scheme or a theme or raid your stash for a totally scrappy look. Play with the number of arcs per block, the bias fabrics, and the final layout. Begin with the Get Started Project on page 31, or expand the idea into a larger quilt.

COOL, CLEAR WATER challenge quilt by Jane Croley, 72″ × 52″

When Jane took on the challenge of taking this pattern and running with it, she wanted to "get out of the box." Jane found eddies and swirls of water in the arcs, so she quickly abandoned her dainty, pastel fabrics. Instead, she assembled a group of fabrics that evoke the feeling of dappled sunlight, rocky eddies, and flowing streams. Jane started with 7 big blocks for a total of 28 individual blocks. She finished the edges with facings instead of binding, so the water keeps flowing right off the quilt. Now Jane will tell you: there is no box!

FABRICATED ENIGMA Joan Metzger, 46½″ × 47″

A collection of fabrics with black, white, and yellow inspired Joan to start her own quilt with arcs. One thing led to another, and soon she was adding hot pink, lime green, and vibrant orange to the mix. Joan turned a mistake into a discovery for the border. By accident, she cut the big block on the diagonal (instead of horizontally and vertically), making four big triangles. The triangles fit perfectly around the sides to make a border.

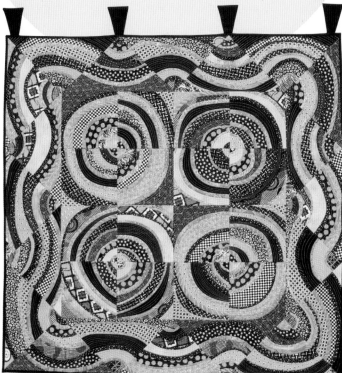

◎ SAMPLE BLOCKS

Let these blocks inspire more ideas about color combinations and looks. The arcs block is a great introduction to bias-covered curves. It's easy, but the results are complex and sophisticated looking. What will you make with the arcs pattern?

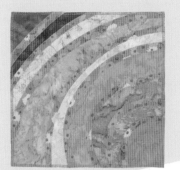

Keep it simple with jewel tones.

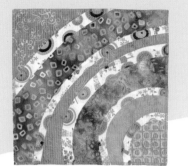

Use light bias fabric.

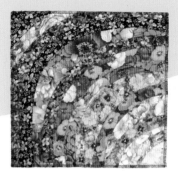

Colorwash arcs.

◎ MAKE IT YOUR OWN

Use the Get Started Project on the next page to make the small quilt or use the directions as guidelines to expand the project. Get inspiration from the quilts and individual blocks for your fabric choices and color schemes. Draw more patterns so each block will be unique. If you like to jump right into a project without planning, just start making blocks and see what happens. It's easy to draw your own big blocks, and you can't go wrong with arcs blocks!

1. Determine the finished size of the individual blocks. Add the seam allowance. Multiply by 2 for the size of the big block. For example, let's say you want the individual block to finish at 6″. Add ½″ for the seam allowance. Multiply 6½″ by 2—the big block is 13″ × 13″.

2. Cut a piece of freezer paper the same size as the big block. Fold the paper in half in both directions to make vertical and horizontal creases. Spread the paper flat again. Starting near the center, draw freehand, loosey-goosey concentric circles.

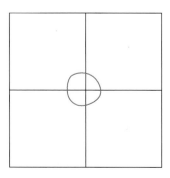

Start first random circle near center.

3. Continue to draw irregular, random concentric circles, right off the edge of the paper.

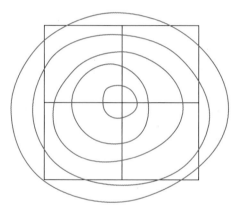

Keep arm loose while drawing.

4. Cut the big block along the fold lines to make 4 individual blocks. Repeat this process until you have enough individual blocks for your project.

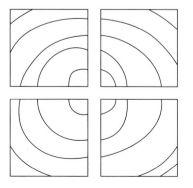

Cut apart on fold lines.

Get Started Project

Review pages 7–13 for basic supplies and techniques.

Drop in the Bucket, Wendy Hill, 19½″ × 19½″; designed by Jane Croley

This is the fun-sized version of *Cool, Clear Water* by Jane Croley (page 29). Just four blocks come together with a swirly motion that could be interpreted in a variety of ways.

◉ SUPPLY LIST

¾ yard Sulky Soft 'n Sheer or other 20″-wide foundation material

Minimum of 10 fat quarters or large scraps of assorted fabrics

½ yard fabric for bias tape

¾ yard fabric for backing

¼ yard fabric for binding (or use several fabrics)

Batting: 24″ × 24″

Thread to match bias tape fabric

Bias makers: ⅜″, ½″, ¾″

Freezer paper

Mechanical pencil

Walking foot

tiP It might be harder than you think to draw random, concentric circles. If you find your circles are too symmetrical, try one of these methods to draw more irregular circles.

- Keep your arm loose and held high in the air, with a light hold on the pencil.

- After drawing the first circle, start at a different point with each additional circle.

- Find a starting point, then close your eyes to draw the circle. Repeat with each circle.

- Use your left hand (if you are right-handed) to draw the circles and vice versa.

- Find a young (and free-spirited) child to draw your circles!

Use a pencil so you can start over. When you are satisfied with your circles, go over the lines with a felt pen.

◉ THE PATTERN

1. Draw 1 big block, 20″ × 20″, on plain paper or directly onto the freezer paper. Fold the paper in half in both directions to make vertical and horizontal creases. Spread the paper flat again.

2. Use a mechanical pencil to freehand draw 7 concentric circles, starting with the inner circle, and roughly following the illustration.

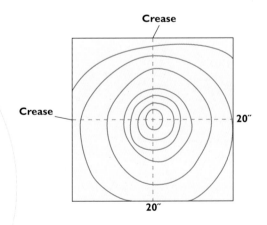

Big block with 7 random concentric circles

3. Cut the big block apart along the fold lines to make 4 individual blocks.

MAKE THE TEMPLATES

1. Trace the 4 block patterns onto freezer paper with the mechanical pencil. (Skip this step if you drew your pattern directly onto the freezer paper.)

2. Cut each block apart into individual arcs. Number the arcs, and keep them paper clipped together. You'll be glad you took these precautions when a burst of air or a playful kitty scatters the pieces!

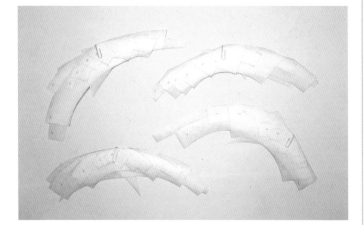

Paper clip arcs together.

CUT OUT THE FABRICS

1. Cut 4 pieces of the foundation material, each 10″ × 10″.

2. Use the templates to cut out the fabrics for each block. Place the waxy side of the template down on the right side of the fabric, and press. Grain line is unimportant because the foundation material supports the fabrics. Cut out the arcs, adding ⅛″ to the outer curve.

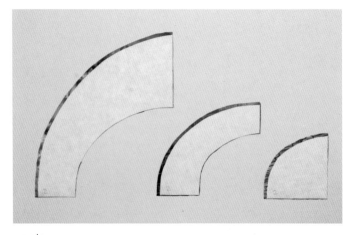

Add ⅛″ to outer curves.

TiP When working with a lot of fabrics, we tend to choose our favorites over and over again without realizing it. The result is not as random looking as hoped for. Force yourself to combine fabrics in new ways. After a piece of fabric has been used, put it in an *off-limits* pile. When all of the fabrics have been used, start over with the entire selection of fabric pieces. The fabrics will be distributed randomly and will look great together.

BUILD THE BLOCKS

1. Assemble the arcs on the foundation material, starting with the smallest (inner) arc. Line up the straight sides, and adjust the arcs as needed to fit the foundation. Pin.

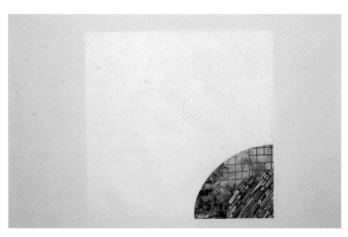

Start with inner quarter-circle.

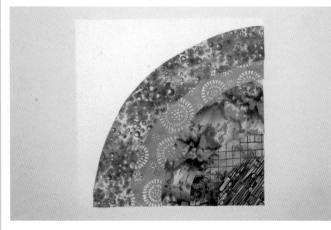

Continue placing arcs in order of size.

Adjust arcs to fit. Pin.

2. Zigzag the curves using a walking foot. Remove the pins as you sew.

3. Repeat Steps 1 and 2 to make a total of 4 blocks.

MAKE THE BIAS TAPE

Review pages 14–17 for making and storing bias tape.

1. Using the ½ yard of fabric for bias, make a batch of ⅜ ″, ½ ″, and ¾ ″ bias tape. Cut 3 strips ¾ ″ wide, 7 strips 1 ″ wide, and 3 strips 1½ ″ wide. Make more bias tape later if needed.

2. Wrap the bias tape around a piece of cardboard, and pin until you are ready to use it.

COVER THE CURVES

Review pages 17–21 for bending, pinning, and stitching the bias tape.

1. Cover the curves with the bias tape. Pin and press to make the bias bend into the curve. Mix up the placement of the different widths of bias tape on each block. Narrow bias tape will bend on any curve; the wider bias tape bends best on more shallow curves. Pin as many curves as possible at once. You want to pin as many as possible at one time, but you don't want so many pins that they interfere with sewing. For this block, you may want to try pinning every other curve.

2. On each strip, stitch the inner curve of the bias first, and then the outer curve, using a walking foot and removing pins as you sew.

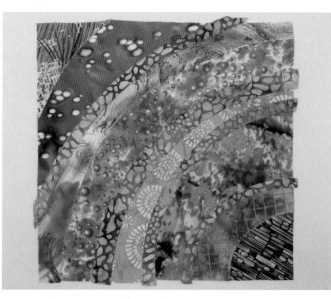

Block in progress

3. Repeat to cover, pin, and stitch all of the curves to make a total of 4 blocks. Trim the excess bias tape even with the sides of the block.

ASSEMBLE THE QUILT TOP

1. Lay out the blocks as shown, or create your own layout.

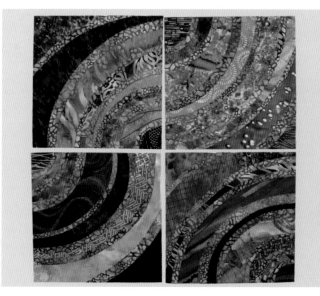

Quilt layout

2. Sew pairs of blocks right sides together into 2 rows. Sew the rows together. Press the seams open or to one side.

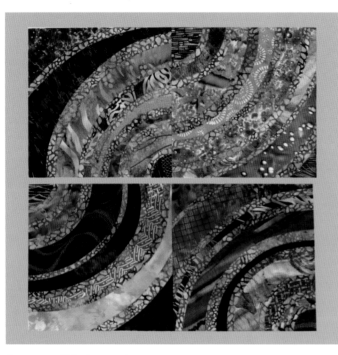

Sew pairs of blocks together.

⊚ FINISH THE QUILT

Review pages 22–26 for quilting, sleeves, binding, and labels.

1. Layer and secure the quilt top with the batting and backing fabric. Quilt the layers together by hand or machine. You might echo the curves, use an overall pattern, or stitch with variegated thread colors.

2. Add a sleeve along the top edge for hanging. Make and attach the binding using one fabric, or piece together several leftovers to add to the flowing feeling of the blocks, as I did. Please add a label to the back of your quilt for family, friends, and quilters today and for curious quilt lovers and historians in the future.

TIP For her large quilt (see page 29), Jane quilted each block before assembly. First she layered each block with batting and backing fabric and then outlined each side of the bias tape with stitching. She then quilted in between, following the curves. After squaring up the blocks, she sewed them right sides together with a $3/8$" seam allowance. Next she pressed the seams open and whipstitched them through the batting just to hold them in place. She covered up the seams with narrow strips of backing fabric, blindstitched by hand through the batting.

One block quilted with batting and backing fabric

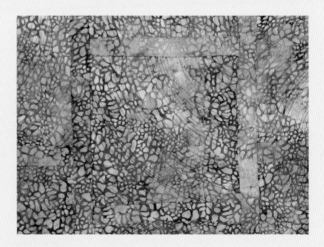

Back of quilt with seam coverings

But Wait, There's More

Quilt patterns with some kind of arc are plentiful. Just about any of these types of patterns can be adapted for bias-covered curves, but I've chosen just four to highlight here. You will apply the same techniques presented in this book to other arc-type patterns. Use freezer-paper templates, build the blocks on a foundation, zigzag the curves, and cover the curves with self-made bias tape. What could be easier?

FREESTYLE ARC BLOCK

This is a simplified version of the Meandering Along pattern, with just 1 random arc. Create the pattern of individual blocks by drawing a big block first, with 2 concentric random circles.

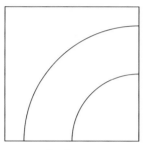

Random arc

NEW YORK BEAUTY

Don't shy away from New York Beauty patterns. By using bias-covered curves, you add another arc to the block pattern and avoid a curved seam at the same time. Assemble the arc with spires by foundation or traditional piecing methods, leaving the seam allowance intact. Cut out the rest of the pattern pieces with no seam allowances on the curves. Build the block on a foundation, and cover the curves with self-made bias tape. It's done!

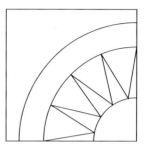

New York Beauty

ANYTHING GOES Wendy Hill, with blocks made by Judi Brown, Christine Hindle Drumright, Pauly Ruth Edwards, Sheila Finzer, Janet Gehlert, Susan Howell, Sarah Kaufman, Beverly King, Crys Kyle, Joan Metzger, Janice Mottau, Dolores Petty, Karla J. Rogers, Linda Saukkonen, and BJ Tinker, 63¾″ × 63¾″; quilted by Linda Bussey

In response to my block challenge, 15 people made 73 blocks with a scrappy color scheme. Sixty of the blocks ended up in the quilt, with the blocks on point.

CHECKERBOARD ARC

Combine bias-covered curve blocks with pieced blocks. Here are 2 examples using simple Four-Patch blocks—find even more for yourself!

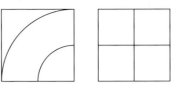

Arc block variation with Four-Patch

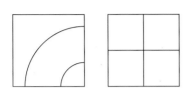

Arc block with Four-Patch

Arcs line up with Four-Patch, resulting in stunning secondary pattern.

Straight furrows layout—arcs overlap

TURN ABOUT

This block appears in many variations and goes by many names, including Orange Peel or Robbing Peter to Pay Paul. This variation is perfect for keeping the arcs out of the seam allowances at the corners of the block. Make this in 2 colors, or spice it up with a contemporary assortment of fabrics.

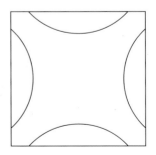

Keep it simple, or spice it up.

tip

Jane used my brainstorming method to fabric shop for her larger version of this quilt, and you can use the same method for your quilts. Brainstorming is a way to generate a variety of options in a short period of time without thinking too much. This is a great method because it's much easier to build a collection by eliminating fabrics from a large group rather than starting with one bolt and painfully working up from there.

Jane wanted the fabrics to enhance her idea for a flowing stream with dappled sunlight and rocky eddies. We gathered up every possible water, sunlight, and rocky-shore fabric in the store. By arranging the fabrics in stacks, Jane could observe the color conversation going on between the fabrics.

Don't think—just grab fabrics as you walk around the store.

Stack up the bolts and watch the color conversation.

Consider the new, revised stack of bolts.

Look at the stack from up close and farther away. Some bolts just won't fit into the group—with their back talking and sassing, they don't add to the color conversation. Remove these fabrics, and check out the new conversation between the remaining bolts of fabric.

Rearranging the stack of bolts allows the colors and textures to collide—just like they will in the finished quilt. Roam through the store again for possible fabrics missed in the first sweep. Add any new bolts that might fit. Pull out bolts that

don't add to the conversation. Keep adjusting until you're satisfied with your fabric collection.

Try new bolts or remove more bolts and observe the color conversation.

Rearrange the same bolts—sometimes this by itself will change your impression of the color conversation.

Look at the stack from a distance as well as up close.

I've heard sculptors say they just chip away everything that doesn't belong. Building a fabric collection using the brainstorming method is similar. You remove the bolts that don't fit in with the color conversation or your ideas. What's left behind is a great group of fabrics, and you can't go wrong with that.

Hint: Generally, fabric store clerks indulge the quilting customer, but there are some ways to stay on their good side. Don't try this method during the annual sale. Do ask which cutting table would be a good place to create the stacks. Do offer to put away the rejected bolts of fabric, even though they'll probably say, "No, thank you." Most importantly, enjoy the process.

Thank you to Jean Wells, Valori Wells, and their staff for helping us photograph at The Stitchin' Post, home of the largest outdoor quilt show, in Sisters, Oregon. Photographs by Craig Howell.

WHiRLiNG SPiRaLS

 Asian-inspired fabrics in both warm and cool colors are striking in these large 12½" blocks. Set together with sashing, the blocks sit side by side. The border repeats the pattern of the sashing with a red square in each of the four corners.

TOKYO TWIST Wendy Hill, 30½" × 30½"

Get to Know the Block

Whirling Spirals, my variation of an old block known as Leatha's Electric Fan, is a surprisingly simple block to make. The fan blades seem to *spin* around the center square. The block construction looks complex, but by using the partial seam technique it's very easy, so don't let its complex look scare you off. Even a beginner can make this block with success.

WHIMSY challenge quilt by Sue McMahan, 59″ × 59″; quilted by Lori Gailey

Sue accepted the challenge to take this pattern idea and run with it using a large block and dotty fabrics. She made sixteen repeat blocks, using an identical fussy-cut center square in each block. Sue amplified the spin found in each block: first, she sewed four blocks together to spin around a new center square, as I did with *Butterfly Breeze*. She then made four large blocks and sewed them together to spin around a final center square. Sue decided to stop here before things really spun out of control!

BUTTERFLY BREEZE Wendy Hill, 26″ × 26″

The pastel fabrics demanded a smaller block, so I made these to finish at 10″ square. Fussy-cut butterflies sit in each center square, surrounded by fresh, breezy pastels in florals, stripes, and dots. Memories of my mother's clothesline blowing in the wind inspired my fabric choices. In this layout, the four blocks spin around a center square cut from a different fabric.

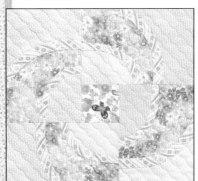

◉ SAMPLE BLOCKS

Here are three more ideas for color combinations and piecing. Whether these blocks are set side by side, with sashing, or in a spin around a center square, Whirling Spirals is a fun pattern to make.

Embellish fan blades before block assembly.

Clockwise fan blades with center circle

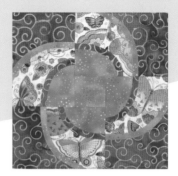

Keep it simple with three fabrics.

◉ MAKE IT YOUR OWN

Now it's your turn to make a Whirling Spirals quilt project. Use the following Get Started Project to make a small quilt, or use this information to create your own variation of the Whirling Spirals pattern.

One block is made up of four repeated rectangle units and a center square. The fan blades can spin clockwise or counter-clockwise.

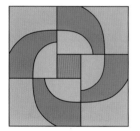   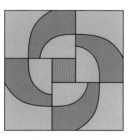

Counterclockwise spin   *Clockwise spin*

To create your own project, review this chapter for inspiration, and decide what you'd like to do. Look at the samples, adjust a little of this or that, and generally add your own ideas. Use the full-size pattern on page 49, or customize it on a photo-copy machine. Enlarge or reduce the pattern in increments of 25% to keep the measurements easy to use. Once you decide on the size of the block, the layout, and the color scheme, you'll be ready to assemble fabrics and supplies.

Get Started Project

Review pages 7–13 for basic supplies and techniques.

A Little Whimsy, Wendy Hill, 32″ × 32″; designed by Sue McMahan

Make this small version in no time. The two different border fabrics add to the fun look of the quilt.

SUPPLY LIST

1½ yards Sulky Soft 'n Sheer or other 20″-wide foundation material

½ yard fabric for block background

½ yard fabric for outer arc

¼ yard fabric for inner arc

⅛ yard fabric for center square

¼ yard fabric for rectangles

¼ yard each of 2 fabrics for border (optional)

½ yard fabric for bias tape

1 yard fabric for backing

⅜ yard fabric for binding

Thread to match bias tape fabric

Batting: 36″ × 36″

Bias makers: ⅜″, ½″

Freezer paper

Mechanical pencil

Walking foot

THE PATTERN

Use the pattern on page 49.

MAKE THE TEMPLATES

1. Trace the pattern onto freezer paper with the mechanical pencil.

2. Cut out the freezer-paper template, and then cut the rectangle apart along the seamlines into the 3 parts: background, outer arc, and inner arc.

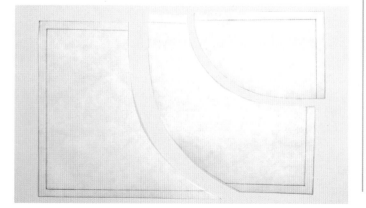

Freezer-paper templates

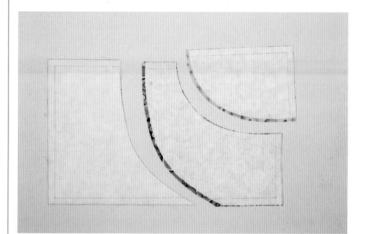

Make multiple templates, and use an assembly-line method to save time when cutting your fabrics. Because there are 4 rectangle units in each block, make 4 rectangle templates, and cut them apart.

CUT OUT THE FABRICS

1. Cut 16 rectangles of the foundation material, each 5½″ × 8″.

2. To cut the backgrounds and arcs, place the freezer-paper templates waxy side down on the right side of the fabric. You'll need 16 pieces of each template. Cut out the shapes, adding ⅛″ to the outer curves.

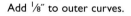

Add ⅛″ to outer curves.

3. Cut 4 center squares, each 3″ × 3″. If you find later on that this fabric seems lightweight when compared with the rectangle units, you can back it with a square of the foundation material. Pin together, and treat as 1 piece when assembling the blocks.

Sue recommends my tip for fussy-cutting without a gridded ruler: To get the starburst in the center of each square, use a freezer-paper template with the seam allowance included.

1. Cut a freezer-paper square 3″ × 3″.

2. Fold the square template twice. Snip the point off the center fold.

3. Use the cut opening and fold lines to precisely place the template.

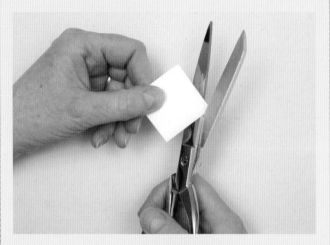

4. Press in place with an iron, and cut along the edges of the freezer paper.

BUILD THE RECTANGLE UNITS

1. Place a rectangle of the Soft 'n Sheer on your work surface. Place the inner arc in the bottom left corner, and pin. Place the outer arc on top, lining up the corner and letting the rest of the arc fall into place. Pin.

2. Place the background piece, and pin, lining up the straight edges on the foundation material.

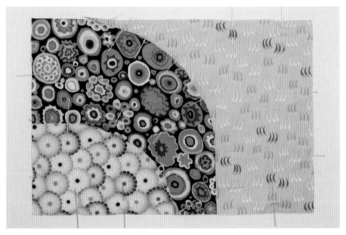

Pin fabrics to foundation.

3. Zigzag the curves, using a walking foot and a narrow but open stitch setting.

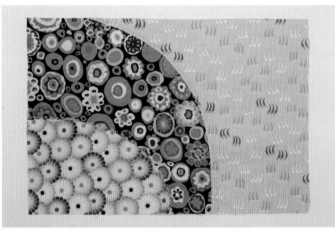

Zigzag curves.

4. Repeat to make a total of 16 rectangle units.

◉ MAKE THE BIAS TAPE

Review pages 14–17 for making and storing bias tape.

1. Using the ½ yard of fabric for the bias, make a batch of ½″ and ⅜″ bias tape. Cut 8 strips 1″ wide and 6 strips ¾″ wide. Make more bias tape later if needed.

2. Wrap the bias tape around a piece of cardboard, and pin until you are ready to use it.

◉ COVER THE CURVES

Review pages 17–21 for bending, pinning, and stitching the bias tape.

1. Cut the ½″-wide bias tape into 16 lengths, each 8½″ long. Cut the ⅜″-wide bias tape into 16 lengths, each 7″ long.

2. Using the ½″ bias on the outer curve and the ⅜″ bias on the inner curve, cover the curves with the bias tape. Pin and press to make the bias tape bend into the curve.

3. Stitch the inner curve first, and then the outer curve, using a walking foot and removing pins as you sew.

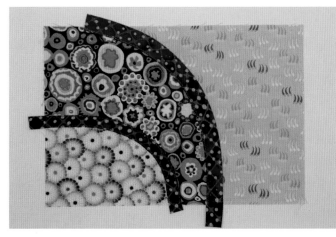

Stitch inner curve of each bias tape first.

4. Repeat to cover and stitch the curves on all 16 of the rectangle units. Trim the ends of the bias even with the straight edge.

◉ ASSEMBLE THE BLOCKS

1. Lay out the parts for 1 block, with all of the units right side up.

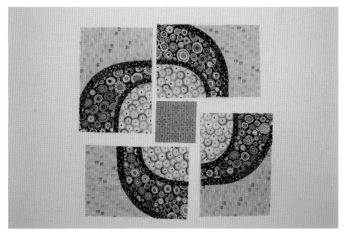

Lay out block.

2. Start with any rectangle. Place the center square right sides together with the rectangle. Pin.

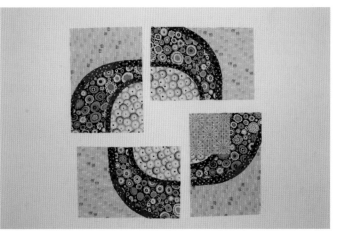

Pin square to rectangle, right sides together.

3. Sew a partial seam from the *middle of* the square to the edge. Backstitch at the start and finish of each seam. Finger-press the seam open. (**Warning:** Pressing with an iron before the block is assembled can distort the block.)

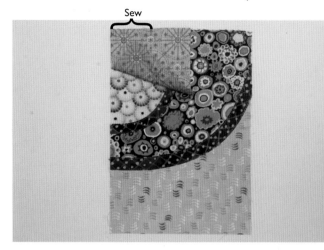

Sew from middle of square to edge.

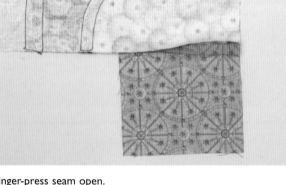

Finger-press seam open.

4. Place the sewn unit back in the layout.

Lay out block again.

5. Place the next rectangle right sides together with the sewn unit. Pin.

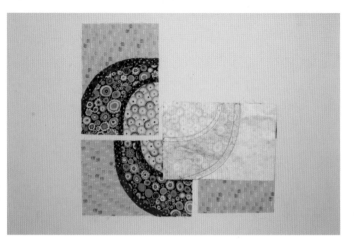

Pin next rectangle in place.

6. Sew the entire seam from one end to the other, backstitching at both ends. Finger-press the seam open.

Finger-pressing prevents distortion.

7. Place the sewn unit back in place in the layout.

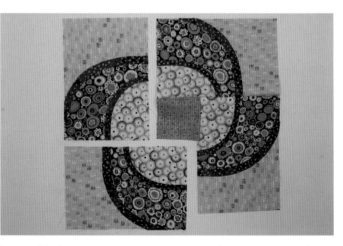

Lay out block once more.

8. Repeat Steps 5, 6, and 7 to sew the next 2 rectangles around the square. Backstitch at both ends of the seams. Finger-press the seams open.

9. To finish the partial seam, place the pieces right sides together, and pin. Sew the seam, starting with the edge and stitching up to the partial seam. Make sure the stitching lines match. Backstitch at both ends. Now use an iron to press all the seams open.

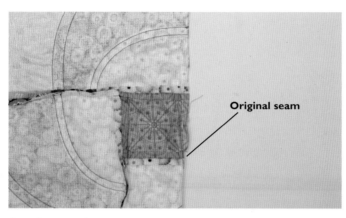

Complete partial seam.

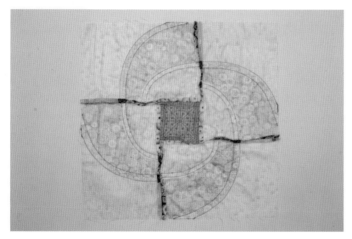

Finger-press seams.

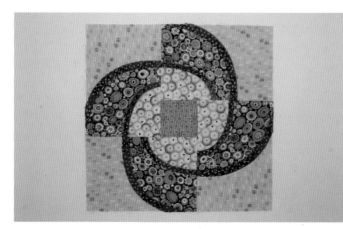

Finished, pressed block

10. Repeat Steps 1–9 to make a total of 4 blocks.

ASSEMBLE THE QUILT TOP

In each block, 4 rectangles spin around the center square. By turning the blocks into rectangles, the new block units can be spun around a new center square. It's easy!

1. From the fabric chosen for the rectangles, cut 2 strips, each 3˝ wide by the width of the fabric, on the crosswise grain. Cut 4 rectangles 3˝ × 13˝ and 1 square 3˝ × 3˝ from the strips.

2. Sew a rectangle to 1 side of each block. Press the seams open.

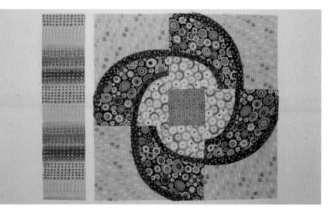

Sew rectangle to block.

3. The sewing process follows the same steps as in assembling a block. Start by laying out the parts.

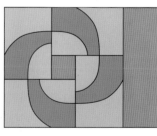

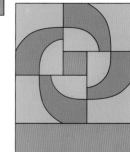

Lay out blocks and center square.

4. Place the center square right sides together with a block unit, and pin. Sew a half seam. Continue adding the block units around the center square, finishing the original half seam at the end. Backstitch all seams. Finger-press as you sew. When finished, press all the seams open with an iron.

5. Leave the quilt top as is, or add a border. I used 2 different border fabrics to continue the spinning effect. Cut 2 strips, each 2½″ wide, on the crosswise grain of each fabric. Pin and sew the border strips to the quilt top in a clockwise direction as you would sew a Log Cabin block. Use a walking foot to feed the layers evenly. Trim each border strip to fit after it is sewn to the quilt top. Press, the seams open or toward the border fabric.

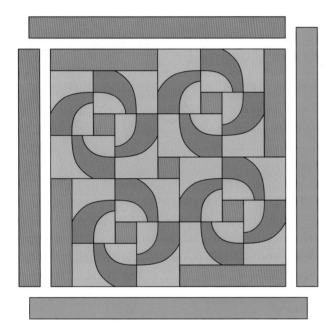

Add borders Log Cabin style.

Turning Blocks into Rectangles

There is a method to the madness of turning square blocks into rectangles. The way the math works, the *width* of the rectangle strips added to the block and the *width* of the new center square must be exactly the same. That makes all the seams on the edges of the block align so that you get a continuous swirl from arc to arc.

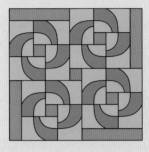

Block side seams line up when all center squares are equal.

Overlap

Block side seams do not meet when new center square is smaller.

Gap

Block side seams "gap" when new center square is larger.

🌀 FINISH THE QUILT

Review pages 22–26 for quilting, sleeves, binding, and labels.

Layer the quilt top with the batting and backing fabric, and secure. Quilt the layers together by hand or by machine. I echo quilted four big quarter-circles on this quilt. I made a quarter-circle freezer-paper template for the first stitched line, then used the walking foot as a guide to echo quilt the remaining lines in each of the four corners.

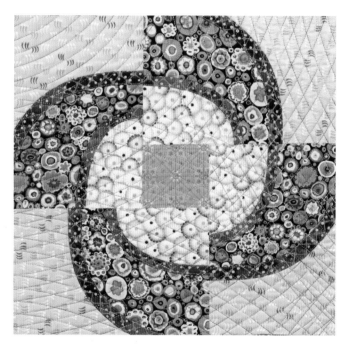

Echo quilting

Add a sleeve along the top edge if you plan to hang the quilt. Bind the edges using your favorite method. Please add a label to the back of your quilt for family, friends, and quilters today and for curious quilt lovers and historians in the future.

But Wait, There's More

I chose four of the many fan block patterns that I researched to include here. They are easily adapted to bias-covered curves. Use a purchased fan block pattern, or draw your own with a protractor and a ruler.

Apply the same techniques used for other blocks in this book. Foundation piece or traditionally piece the fan blades together. Then, using freezer-paper templates, build the blocks on a foundation, zigzag the curves, and cover the curves with self-made bias tape. It's as easy as that!

🌀 BASIC FAN BLOCK

I could spend a year working with even the basic fan block and never make the same quilt twice. Maybe I will!

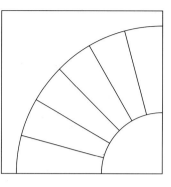

Fan block with three parts

🌀 DOUBLE FAN BLOCK

Arranged side by side, these double fan blocks create exciting secondary patterns. The fans may be the same size or different sizes.

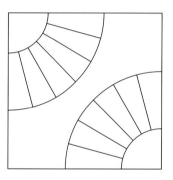

Equal-size double fans

🌀 STARBURST FAN

This block, with the fan in the background area, goes by many names. Think sunshine, rainbows, color-themed blocks, color with black-and-white prints, and more!

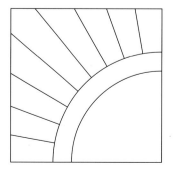

So many possibilities!

◉ HALF-CIRCLE FAN BLOCKS

This illustration shows 12 fan blades, but it could be drafted with 6 or 9 fan blades. Play with the layout to make whole circles, wavy lines, or do what Joan did with her quilt shown below.

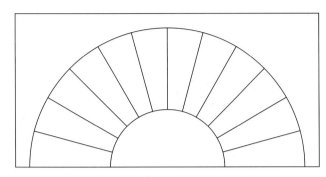

Half-circle fan block with twelve blades

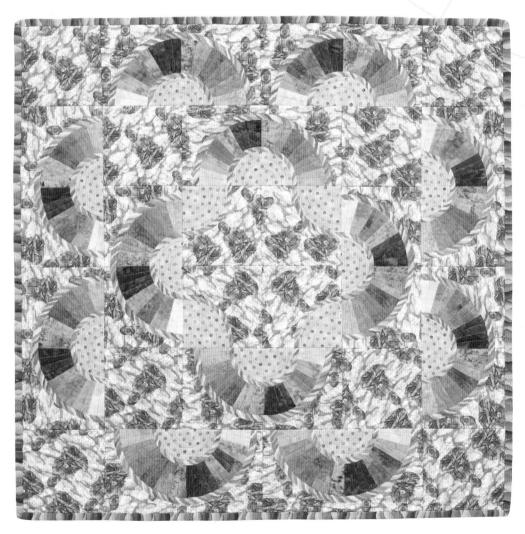

SOMEWHERE... Joan Metzger, 37″ × 37″

Joan fell in love with a half-circle New York Beauty pattern from a magazine that is more than 100 years old. She replaced the original pieced arcs with plain fan blades. Joan used fabrics from several Timeless Treasures collections.

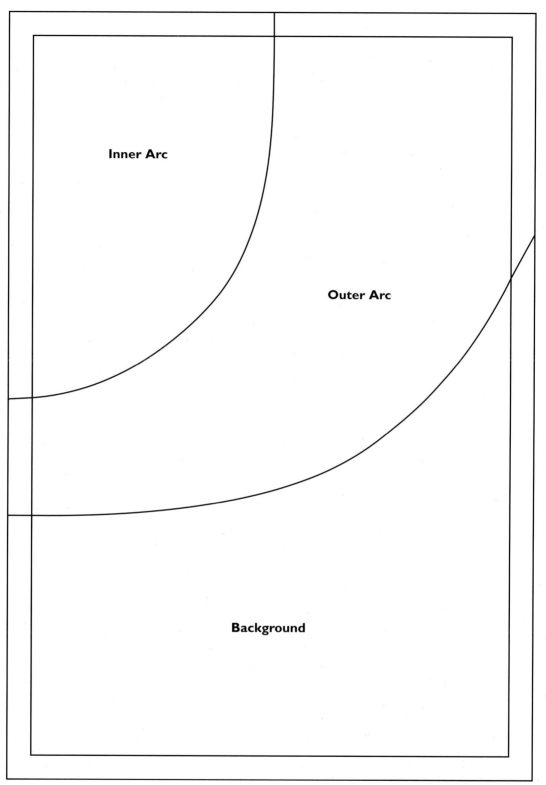

Inner Arc

Outer Arc

Background

Cut 16 of each.

Finished block: 12½″; pattern includes seam allowance

Make 4 for each block.

WHiRLYGiGGiNG

Millefleur—a thousand flowers—inspired this quilt. Mosaic fabrics in a variety of styles and colors worked beautifully with my idea for the hexagons. Although the hexagon shape stands out, the quilt top is easily pieced together in horizontal rows.

TUTTI FRUITI Wendy Hill, 36½″ × 35¼″

Get to Know the Block

I call this pattern WhirlyGigging, a name to cover all the variations of this old traditional block. The construction process begins with triangles—eight for a square or rectangular block and six for a hexagon block. The petal shapes can spin in either direction. With bias-covered curves, this block is a cinch to make.

WHIRLYGIGS challenge quilt by Carol Loehndorf-Webb, 35½″ × 50″

Within hours of accepting the challenge to take my pattern and run with it, Carol sketched a plan for making whirlygig blocks in different sizes. Next Carol made a variety of blocks, all without templates. One day she said, "Enough," and started piecing the quilt top together. Carol intentionally let some blocks come forward and let others melt into the background.

DAY & NIGHT IN THE GARDEN Wendy Hill, 28¼″ × 29″

Bright yellows, blues, and greens really warm up our house, especially in winter. I let the quilt evolve as I worked, but I knew the 6″ and 12″ blocks would fit together in a variety of layout options. Extra half-blocks found their way into the border, along with leftovers too small to use any other way. The repeat blocks add stability to this otherwise spontaneous quilt.

 SAMPLE BLOCKS

Here are more ideas for whirligigs in a variety of sizes, shapes, and color combinations.

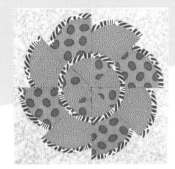

Hexagon block with long, graceful petals

Double whirlygig

Generous, round petals with center circle

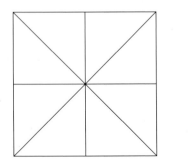 MAKE IT YOUR OWN

Think about making your own WhirlyGigging project. Use the following Get Started Project to make a small quilt, or adjust the information to make one of your own design. Make one block, or make a dozen or more! It's easy to create your own pattern. Start with a square or rectangle; divide it first horizontally and vertically, and then diagonally to make eight triangles. Add the petal shapes by freehand drawing each one or by repeating the same petal shape.

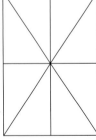

Square or rectangle block

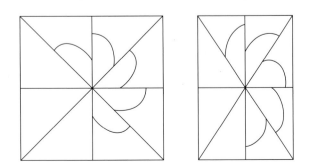

Add petal shapes.

Hexagons are just as easy to draw if you start with equilateral triangle graph paper. Divide the hexagon into 6 triangles. Add the petal shapes.

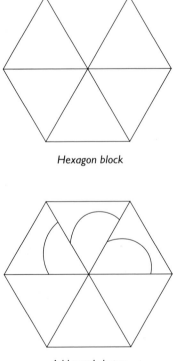

Hexagon block

Add petal shapes.

It's great as a repeat block with a scrappy or a set color scheme. Make blocks in a variety of sizes, and then fit them together like puzzle pieces. Repeat an identical petal shape in each triangle, or allow each petal shape to be unique. Or try them all.

Get Started Project

Review pages 7–13 for basic supplies and techniques.

Whirlygig, Carol Loehndorf-Webb, 19½″ × 19½″

◎ SUPPLY LIST

1¼ yards Sulky Soft 'n Sheer or other 20″-wide foundation material

⅛ yard fabric for first (inner) petal

¼ yard fabric for second petal

¼ yard fabric for third petal

¾ yard fabric for background

¼ yard fabric #1 for bias tape (first petal)

¼ yard fabric #2 for bias tape (second petal)

⅓ yard fabric #3 for bias tape (third petal)

⅔ yard fabric for backing

⅜ yard fabric for binding

Batting: 24″ × 24″

Thread to match bias tape fabrics

Bias makers: ½″, ¾″

Freezer paper

Mechanical pencil

Walking foot

◎ THE PATTERN

1. Draw a square, 10⅜″ × 10⅜″, on plain paper or directly onto the freezer paper. This will create one quarter of the block—1 block unit. Draw a diagonal line from corner to corner. Use a mechanical pencil so you can erase and make changes if needed.

2. Freehand draw 3 arcs in each triangle, roughly following the diagrams. Make each triangle slightly different for variety.

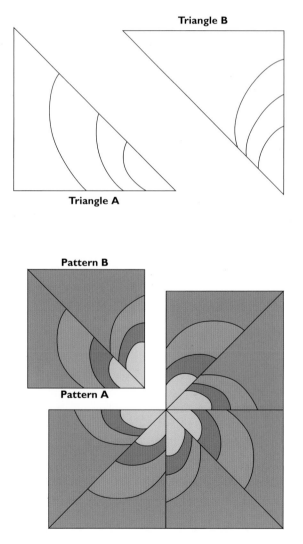

Construction outline: each finished block unit is 9½″ × 9½″; the finished block is 19″ × 19″.

MAKE THE TEMPLATES

1. Trace the 2 patterns onto the freezer paper with the mechanical pencil. (Skip this step if you drew your pattern directly onto the freezer paper.)

2. Cut out the triangle templates. Cut each triangle apart into the component parts. Number the parts and use a paper clip to keep the parts of each triangle together until you are ready to use them.

tip Carol likes to use freehand construction for each triangle. Make a template of the entire triangle, including seam allowances. Cut the foundation material about 1" larger than the triangle template. Beginning with the inner petal, freehand cut this petal shape, and place it on the foundation material. Slide the next fabric under the first petal, and freehand cut the top of the petal. Keep going with the next two fabrics.

Slide next fabric underneath.   Freehand cut top of petal.

Zigzag the raw edges. Make bias tape. Carol prefers to make hand-folded bias tape without the use of bias maker gadgets (see pages 16–17).

Cover the curves with the bias tape, and stitch in place. Cut out the finished triangle using the triangle template. Repeat this process to make a total of 8 triangles. Each will be slightly different.

CUT OUT THE FABRICS

1. Cut 4 squares of the foundation material, each 10⅜" × 10⅜". Cut each square on the diagonal once to make a total of 8 triangles.

2. Use the templates to cut out the fabrics for each triangle unit. Place the waxy side of the freezer-paper template down on the right side of the fabric, and press. Cut out 8 pieces of fabric with each template, adding ⅛" to the outer curves. Grain line is unimportant because the foundation supports the fabrics.

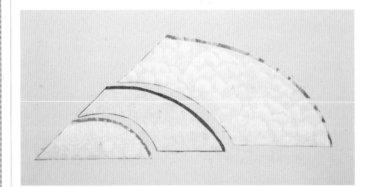

Add ⅛" to outer curves.

BUILD THE BLOCKS

1. Assemble the petals on the foundation triangles, starting with the smallest (inner) petal. Keep adding petals, lining up the straight sides and adjusting to fit as needed. Pin.

2. Zigzag the curves, using a walking foot and removing pins as you sew.

Triangle unit in progress

3. Repeat Steps 1 and 2 to construct a total of 8 triangles (4 each of the A and B triangles).

◎ MAKE THE BIAS TAPE

Review pages 14–17 for making and storing bias tape.

1. Make a batch of ½″ bias tape using fabrics #1 and #2 by cutting 8 strips, 1″ wide from each. Make ¾″ bias tape with fabric #3 by cutting 8 strips 1½″ wide. Make more bias tape later if needed.

2. Wrap the bias tape around a piece of cardboard, and pin until you are ready to use it.

◎ COVER THE CURVES

Review pages 17–21 for bending, pinning, and stitching the bias tape.

1. Use bias made from fabric #1 to cover the first (inner) curve on each triangle. Use bias from fabric #2 to cover the second curve and from fabric #3 to cover the last (outer) curve. Pin and press to make the bias tape bend into the curve.

2. Stitch the inner curve first, and then the outer curve, using a walking foot and removing pins as you sew.

Finished triangle units

◎ ASSEMBLE THE QUILT TOP

1. Arrange the 8 triangles on the work surface to form a large square.

Arrange pieces.

2. Sew 2 pairs of triangles right sides together to make a smaller square block. Press the seams open. Repeat to make a total of 4 square blocks.

3. Sew the blocks right sides together in pairs to make 2 rows.

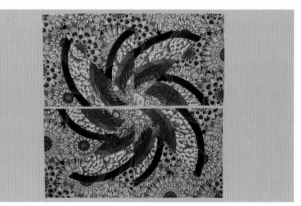

Assemble blocks.

4. Sew the 2 rows right sides together, matching up the seams at the intersection.

Finished quilt top

◎ FINISH THE QUILT

Review pages 22–26 for quilting, sleeves, binding, and labels.

1. Layer the quilt top with the batting and backing fabric, and secure. Quilt the layers together by hand or machine. Echo quilt around the Whirlygigs with a walking foot as Carol did, or use your own quilting ideas.

Echo quilting around Whirlygig

2. Add a sleeve along the top edge for hanging. Bind the edges using your favorite method. Please add a label to the back of your quilt for family, friends, and quilters today and for curious quilt lovers and historians in the future.

But Wait, There's More

With bias-covered curves, the door is opened to all sorts of related patterns using triangles and petal shapes too daunting to piece. Apply the same techniques presented in this section to make the following blocks. Use freezer-paper templates, build the blocks on a foundation, zigzag the curves, and cover the curves with bias tape. Quilts with curves? No problem!

◎ PINWHEEL WHIRLYGIGS

In this version of Whirlygigs, 4 of the triangles have elongated petals and 4 have quarter-circles. It's easy to make but you don't have to admit this when people rave about your quilt. Make it as a repeat block, or use a lot of fabrics.

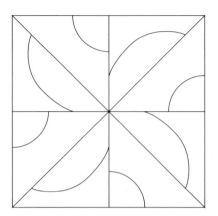

Combine petals and quarter-circles.

Photo by Craig Howell

Windmills, Susan Howell, 32¾″ × 40¼″; a baby quilt for Brooklyn Eve Sams, October 9, 2005

FLOWER POWER

Equilateral triangles make a great shape for placing petals in the corners. The fun begins in the secondary pattern when the rows of triangles are assembled. Plan the layout ahead of time or not—let random patterns just happen. It might even be fun to leave a petal out here and there (he loves me, he loves me not).

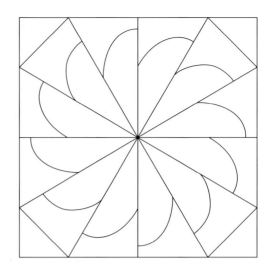

Sunburst variation

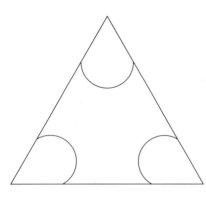

One triangle shape

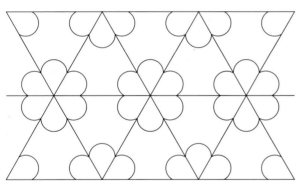

Great secondary pattern

SUNBURST VARIATION

This block looks complicated, but when broken down into bias-covered curve parts, it's easier than you think. Divide each square into 3 equal parts (30° and 60° angles), and use a protractor or compass to draw the curves. Add the corner triangles using the shortcut method with squares—draw a diagonal line from corner to corner on the wrong side of the square, layer it on the corner, sew on the drawn line, trim the corner leaving a ¼″ seam allowance, and press.

ROSE PETALS

This rose variation would make a great repeat block or a wonderful addition to a flower sampler quilt. Constructed with just 3 templates and 4 triangles, it goes together quickly.

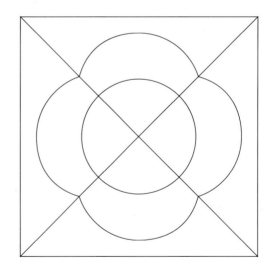

Rose petals

CUTTING CORNERS

A large collection of pink, orange, and yellow fabrics inspired this quilt. I just had to use them all, so I strip pieced the backgrounds of the quarter-circle blocks. With the blocks set on point, the pattern looks more complicated than it is. It's simply big blocks made up of sixteen quarter-circle units.

GIRLIE GIRL Wendy Hill, 56″ × 56″; quilted by Linda Bussey

Get to Know the Block

Cutting Corners is my name for a large group of patterns using quarter-circles. You know this pattern by many names, usually depending on the value placement and layout: Drunkard's Path, Snowball, Fool's Puzzle, and the list goes on. Each block is composed of two pieces with one bias-covered curve. Simple to construct, this block can entertain us until the cows come home.

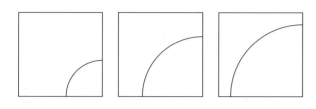

Quarter-circle block in different sizes

Perhaps this block should be called a chameleon, since quilts made with this block don't look alike until closer examination. Get going with the Get Started Project on page 60, or use the inspiration of the quilts and blocks to create your own quilt.

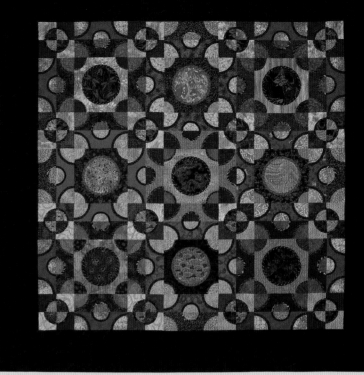

AKA NO IN-EI (Shades of Red), challenge quilt by Kathy H. Shaker, 83″ × 83″; quilted by Linda Bussey

Kathy knew right away she wanted to tap into her red fabric stash when she took on the challenge of taking my pattern ideas and running with them. Kathy expanded the block I used for *Girlie Girl* to include quarter-, half-, and whole circles. After finishing one block, Kathy found herself making more and more blocks. She stopped at nine blocks, after using 90 different red fabrics. Some quilts are like that—they just keep growing!

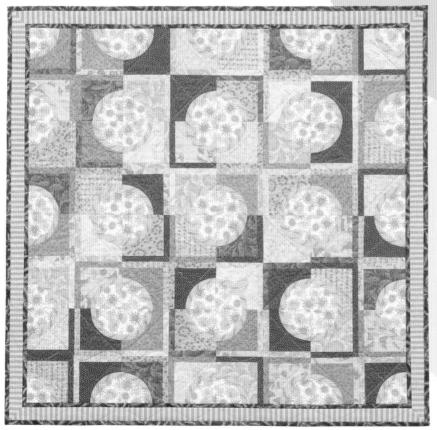

IN THE WOODS Wendy Hill, 40¾″ × 40¾″

After I finished *Girlie Girl*, I found another pink, yellow, and orange fabric. I decided to take the quilt in another color direction with assorted greens and browns. Contemporary screen prints, Civil War reproduction fabrics, batiks—this is a melting pot of fabric styles with color the common link. The clerk at the fabric store told me the fabrics couldn't possibly go together. What do you think?

◎ SAMPLE BLOCKS

For each of the sample blocks, I used the same two-by-two block setting, for easy comparison of the color combinations.

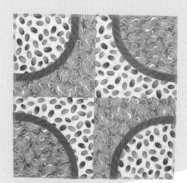
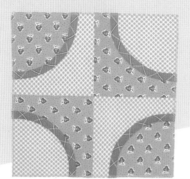
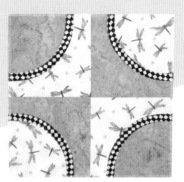

Taupe fabrics create subtle effect.　　Complementary colors in pumpkin and Dutch blue　　Fun novelty fabrics with black/white check

◎ MAKE IT YOUR OWN

Perhaps you've always wanted to play around with quarter-circle blocks and the seemingly infinite layout patterns, such as Drunkard's Path. It's easy to draw your own pattern. First, determine the size of the square. Then add the quarter-circle.

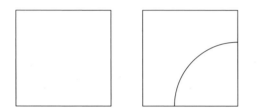

Start with square; add quarter-circle.

If you have a compass, use it to draw the quarter-circle. If not, you can easily arrive at a quarter-circle by tracing around a bowl or plate. Cut out the circle, and fold it in half twice. Use this quarter-circle as a guide for drawing the quarter-circle pattern. (Vary the size of the quarter-circle by starting with different size bowls and plates.)

I bet you can't wait to make your own Cutting Corners quilt. Use the following Get Started Project to make a small quilt like Kathy's, using one big block and a pieced border. If you get carried away as Kathy did, keep making the big blocks until you have enough. Add the pieced border to the assembled big blocks to finish the pattern. Refer to the Fabric Placement Diagram; the block is outlined in bold.

Get Started Project

Review pages 7–13 for basic supplies and techniques.

Really Red, Wendy Hill, 28½″ × 28½″; designed by Kathy H. Shaker

◉ SUPPLY LIST

Note: You will need 5 fabrics for the circles and 5 fabrics for the backgrounds.

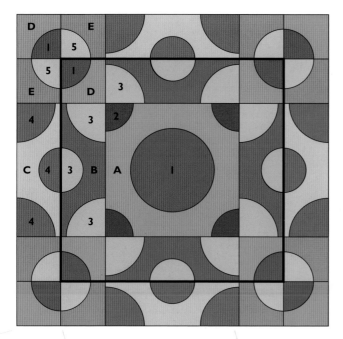

Fabric Placement Diagram

⅜ yard fabric #1

⅛ yard fabric #2

¼ yard fabric #3

¼ yard fabric #4

⅛ yard fabric #5

½ yard fabric A

⅜ yard fabric B

⅜ yard fabric C

¼ yard fabric D

¼ yard fabric E

½ yard fabric for bias tape

1 yard fabric for backing

⅜ yard fabric for binding

Batting: 33″ × 33″

Thread to match bias tape fabric

Bias makers: ⅜″, ½″

Freezer paper

Mechanical pencil

Walking foot

◉ THE PATTERN

Use a compass to draw the circles and a ruler to divide them. You can draw the circles on plain paper or directly onto the freezer paper.

- Draw 1 circle with an 8″ diameter (4″ radius).

- Draw 1 circle with a 4″ diameter (2″ radius), and draw a line to cut it in half.

- Draw 1 circle with a 7½″ diameter (3¾″ radius), and draw 2 lines to cut it in quarters.

- Draw 1 circle with a 5¾″ diameter (2⅞″ radius), and draw 2 lines to cut it in quarters.

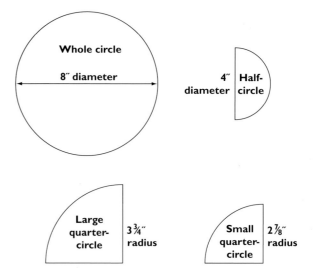

Whole, half-, and quarter-circles

For this project, the blocks are built right on the cut squares and rectangles (not on a separate foundation material). Use templates to cut the quarter-, half- and whole circles. Use the measurements given on page 62 to cut the background squares and rectangles. After the bias tape is stitched in place, you can cut away the excess fabric from the back.

◎ MAKE THE TEMPLATES

1. Trace the whole, half- and quarter-circle patterns onto freezer paper with a mechanical pencil. (Skip this step if you drew the patterns directly onto the freezer paper.)

2. Cut out the freezer-paper templates along the lines.

 **tip** Make multiple templates to save time. Make 4 templates each of the half- and quarter-circles.

◎ CUT OUT THE FABRICS

1. Use the templates and the fabric placement diagram (page 61) to cut the following pieces; do not add 1/8″ around the curves. Place the waxy side of the template down on the right side of the fabric. Press lightly with a warm iron. After cutting out the fabric shapes, peel off and reuse the templates.

Fabric #1: 1 large circle and 8 small quarter-circles

Fabric #2: 4 small quarter-circles

Fabric #3: 8 large quarter-circles and 4 half-circles

Fabric #4: 8 large quarter-circles and 4 half-circles

Fabric #5: 8 small quarter-circles

2. Use the fabric placement diagram and the following measurements to cut the backgrounds.

Fabric A: 1 large square, 12½″ × 12½″

Fabric B: 4 rectangles, 4½″ × 12½″

Fabric C: 4 rectangles, 4½″ × 12½″

Fabric D: 8 small squares, 4½″ × 4½″

Fabric E: 8 small squares, 4½″ × 4½″

 tip Kathy treated her cut fabrics with spray starch to stiffen them. That made the pieces easy to handle when covering the curves and assembling the quilt top. Follow the directions on the product, and always test on a small piece of fabric. Wash out the spray starch after the quilting is completed. Kathy says for everything else "there's chocolate."

◎ BUILD THE BLOCKS

Refer to the fabric placement diagram on page 61 to build the units. The background pieces serve as the foundation for placing the whole, half-, and quarter-circles.

CENTER SQUARE

1. Center the large circle in the middle of the large square, and pin. Place the 4 small Fabric #2 quarter-circles in the corners, and pin, lining up the sides.

2. Zigzag the curves, using a walking foot and removing the pins as you sew.

Zigzagged center square

RECTANGLES

1. Use the rectangles cut from Fabric B to make 1 set of 4 rectangle units. Center the Fabric #3 half-circle along one long edge, and pin. Place the large Fabric #3 quarter-circles in the opposite corners, and pin, lining up the side raw edges. Repeat to assemble 4 rectangle units all at one time.

2. Zigzag the curves, using a walking foot and removing pins as you sew.

3. Repeat Steps 1 and 2 to assemble the remaining set of 4 rectangle units from Fabric C and the Fabric #4 quarter- and half-circles, for a total of 8.

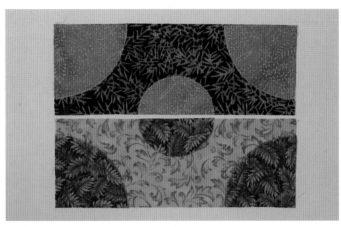

One each of 2 rectangle units

SQUARES

1. Use the squares cut from Fabric D to make 1 set of 8 small square units. Place the small Fabric #1 quarter-circles in a corner of each square, and pin, lining up the side raw edges. Prepare 8 square units.

2. Zigzag the curves, using a walking foot and removing pins as you sew.

3. Repeat Steps 1 and 2 using the Fabric E squares and the Fabric #5 quarter-circles. You will have a total of 16 square units.

One each of 2 square units

◉ MAKE THE BIAS TAPE

Review pages 14–17 for making and storing bias tape.

For a scrappy look, use several fabrics for the bias tape, or follow the directions for using just one fabric.

1. Make a batch of ³⁄₈″ and ½″ bias tape using your chosen fabric. Cut 8 strips ¾″ wide and 6 strips 1″ wide. Make more bias tape later if needed.

2. For the continuous loop of ½″ bias tape that will cover the center circle, cut 2 strips 1″ wide. Sew them together to make a long strip by placing the ends right sides together, marking the diagonal seam, and stitching along the line. Trim the excess, leaving a ¼″ seam allowance. Press the seam open, and baste before making the bias tape. Set aside for later. (See page 64.)

3. Wrap the bias tape around a piece of cardboard, and pin until you are ready to use it.

◉ COVER THE CURVES

Review pages 17–21 for bending, pinning, stitching, and making continuous loops of bias.

1. Use the ½″ bias tape to cover the large quarter-circles on the rectangle units. Cut 16 segments, each 7″ long. Cover the curves; pin and press to make the bias bend into the curve. Stitch the bias tape in place, starting with the inner curve first.

2. Use the ³⁄₈″ bias tape on the half- and small quarter-circles. For the half-circles, cut 8 segments, each 7¼″ long. For the small quarter-circles, cut 20 segments, each 5¾″ long. Cover the curves; pin and press to make the bias bend into the curve. Stitch the bias tape in place, starting with the inner curve first.

3. Trim off the ends of the bias tape even with the sides of the units.

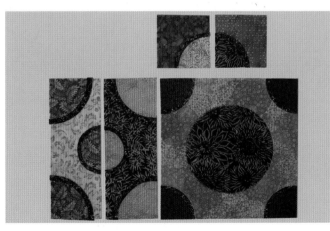

Finished units

4. To make the continuous loop of ½" bias tape, use the seamed piece already set aside. Cut the bias tape 26¾" long. You might want to measure the circumference of your circle first to double-check the length. It's better if your loop is a bit long, rather than too short. (Refer to Whole Circles on pages 18–21 for further instructions.) Place the ends right sides together, mark the diagonal seam, and stitch along the marked line. Trim the excess fabric, leaving a ¼" seam allowance. Press the seam open, and refold the bias tape.

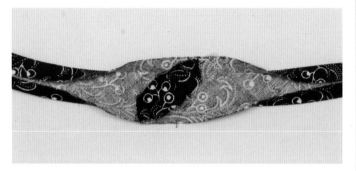

Stitched diagonal seam

5. Fold the loop of bias tape in half twice, and mark the quarter points with pins. Fold the freezer-paper template for the large circle into fourths. Use the fold lines to mark the quarter points on the fabric circle with pins.

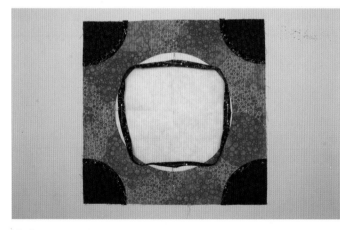

Mark quarter points.

6. Remove the freezer-paper template. Pin the bias tape loop to the circle, matching up the pins on both. Ease in the bias tape between the pins, using 1 or 2 additional pins in each quarter. Adjust as needed to make the bias tape round and smooth looking. Mist with water, and lightly press to bend the bias tape into the curve.

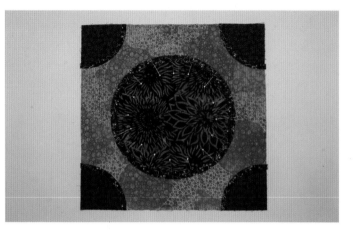

Pin bias tape loop to circle.

7. Stitch the bias loop in place, starting with the inner circle first, using a walking foot and removing pins as you sew.

8. Carefully cut away the excess fabric on the back, leaving a ⅛" to ¼" seam allowance.

ASSEMBLE THE QUILT TOP

1. Refer to the quilt photo on page 60 and the fabric placement diagram on page 61 to lay out the units for assembly.

2. Sew a pair of rectangle units right sides together, lining up the bias tape of the half-circles. Press the seams open. Repeat Step 1 to assemble a total of 4 rectangle units.

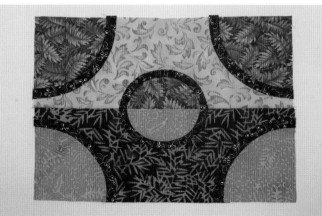

Line up bias tape. Sew.

3. Sew a pair of square units together, lining up the bias tape of the quarter-circles. Press the seams open. Repeat to assemble a total of 8 pairs of units.

Line up bias tape; sew.

4. Complete the corner unit by sewing the pairs from Step 3 together, lining up the bias tape of the quarter-circles. Press the seams open. Repeat to assemble a total of 4 square units.

Line up bias tape; sew.

5. Sew a rectangle unit to opposite sides of the center square. Press the seams open.

Partially assembled quilt top

6. Place 1 square unit right sides together on each end of a rectangle unit. Sew together. Press the seams open. Repeat to make a total of 2 units.

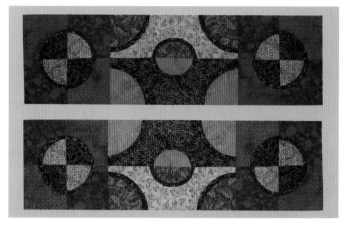

Top and bottom completed

7. Sew the 2 rectangle units from Step 6 to the top and bottom of the center piece. Press the seams open.

◉ FINISH THE QUILT

Review pages 22–26 for quilting, sleeves, binding, and labels.

1. Layer the quilt top with the batting and backing fabric, and secure. Quilt the layers together by hand or machine. Use a grid pattern as I did, or use your own quilting ideas.

Wavy-line grid quilting

2. Add a sleeve along the top edge for hanging the quilt. Bind the edges using your favorite method. Please add a label to the back of your quilt for family, friends, and quilters today and for curious quilt lovers and historians in the future.

But Wait, There's More

Quarter-circle blocks can be found in dozens (and dozens) of traditional patterns, used alone or in combination with pieced units. There are enough options to last a lifetime, but I've chosen four of my favorites to share with you.

◉ RING OR CHAIN

Just 1 quarter-circle block creates this pattern—with planned value, color, or fabric placement.

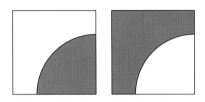

One block, two value/color/fabric placements

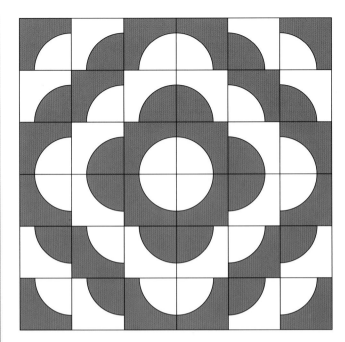

Continue layout pattern for larger quilt.

This quilt features neutral and 1930s reproduction fabrics. Fifteen people contributed 180 blocks in response to my block challenge. This block is so much fun to make, it would be easy to make all the blocks yourself. In fact, I'm going to have to make one for *myself*!

Photo by Sharon Risedorph

FRIENDSHIP RING Wendy Hill, with blocks made by Carol J. Born, Diana Bos, Judi Brown, Christine Hindle Drumright, Carole Elsbree, Janet Gehlert, Susan Howell, Sarah Kaufman, Beverly King, Mary Klein, Joan Metzger, Karla J. Rogers, Linda Saukkonen, and Kathy H. Shaker, 60½″ × 80¾″; quilted by Linda Bussey

◎ DOUBLE THE FUN

Put quarter-circle blocks in opposite corners. Make the quarter-circles identical or of different sizes. Either way, used alone or in combination with a half-square triangle block, the secondary patterns are fantastic.

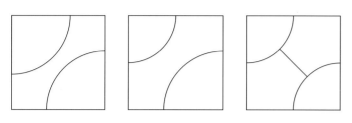

Variations

◎ MAKE A WISH

Combine quarter blocks with pieced blocks—a dynamite combination no matter which layout you choose. Here is the 2-block combo with one layout option.

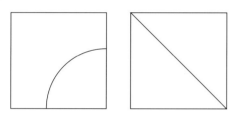

Two-block combination

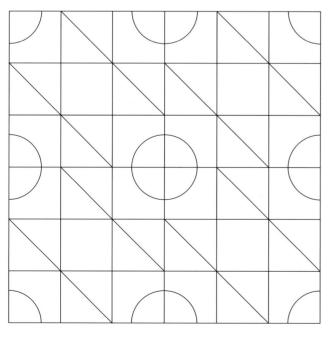

Layout option

◎ PUZZLE

This is an old block made new with bias-covered curves. The triangles and curves in each unit make wonderful secondary patterns when assembled.

Unit

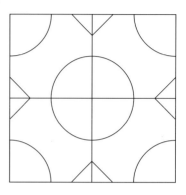

Block

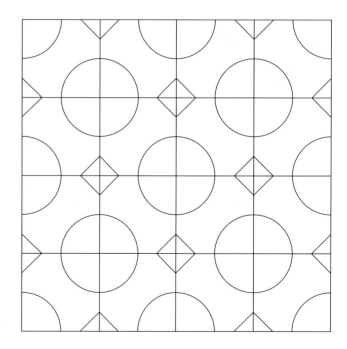

Layout option

Making the Rounds

This simple repeated pattern consists of 30 small whole circles in 13 different colors of silk fabric. A pieced border of half-squares frames the quilt. These silk fabrics unraveled just sitting in the plastic bag, so I fused a lightweight tricot knit interfacing to the reverse side of the silk. That solved the problem without adding noticeable weight or stiffness. The small continuous loops of silk bias tape were bent into submission on paper first before using them to cover the curves (see pages 18–21).

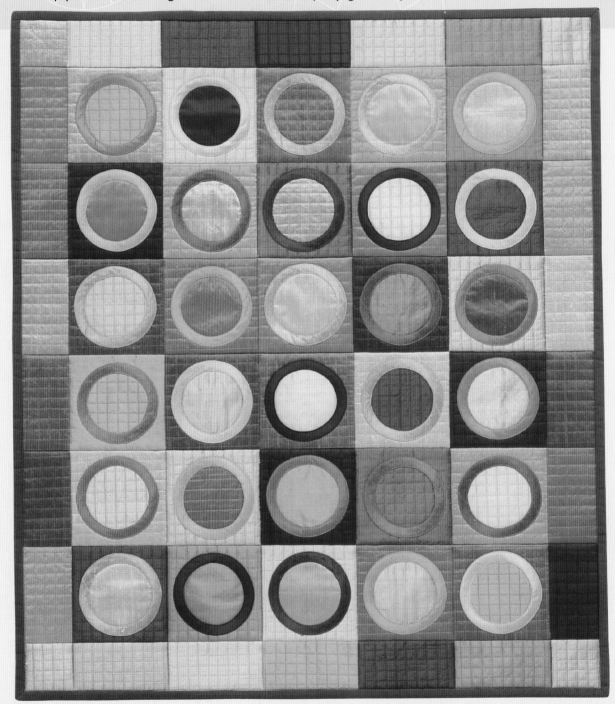

AROUND AND ABOUT Wendy Hill, 27½″ × 31½″

Get to Know the Block

This is an open-ended invitation to play with whole circles. The key is what you do with the circles: adapt traditional patterns, foundation piece the rings first, or cluster whole circles on a background. With bias-covered curves you can tackle any of those options with ease.

AROUND AND AROUND WE GO challenge quilt by Susan Howell, 52¼″ × 52¼″

Susan played around with a lot of ideas after accepting the challenge to take the idea of whole circles and run with it. Finally it was the fabrics she fell in love with at the store that guided her overall design. She pieced the background first, knowing she would somehow cluster various sizes of whole circles over it. Susan created numerous circles first, and then auditioned their placement on her design wall. Digital cameras make it easy to keep an instant record of different layouts. Susan was pleasantly surprised to find that it didn't take long at all to cover the curves with continuous bias tape loops.

RINGS Wendy Hill, 24¾″ × 24¾″

I sketched the concentric rings on freezer paper, keeping my arm loose to draw circles that are somewhat irregular in shape. The freezer-paper rings became templates to cut out the foundation material. The two inner circles are simply cut from interesting fabrics. I foundation pieced the two outer rings on the permanent foundation. After assembling the circles on the background fabric and covering the curves, I decided to add a randomly pieced border just for the fun of it. Echo quilting lines in concentric rings (created using a walking foot) carry the theme throughout the quilt.

◎ SAMPLE BLOCKS

Here are more ideas for whole circles. For easy comparison of the various fabric combinations, I used a simple bull's-eye pattern.

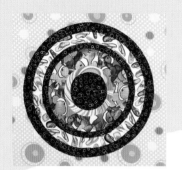

Fun novelty fabrics make you smile.

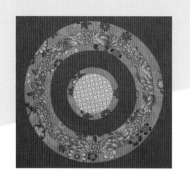

Muted plum, pumpkin, and blue glow.

Combine textures for a captivating look.

◎ MAKE IT YOUR OWN

Now it's your turn to make a whole-circle quilt. A good way to begin is to make the small quilt found in the following Get Started Project, with clustered whole circles on a pieced background. If you get hooked and want to continue working with whole circles, check out the additional patterns at the end of the chapter, and look through pattern books for blocks with whole circles. In no time, you'll be able to put together a little of this and that to create your own project.

Get Started Project

Review pages 7–13 for basic supplies and techniques.

Around and Around We Go Again, Susan Howell, 36½″ × 36½″

◉ SUPPLY LIST

Note: In the quilt shown, fabric #1 is a multicolor print, fabric #2 is light gray, and fabric #3 is dark gray.

1¼ yards fabric #1 for background

⅜ yard fabric #2 for sashing

⅝ yard fabric #3 for contrast sashing and border

Scraps of 25 or more assorted fabrics for circles

10 or more assorted fabrics, at least 18″ × 20″, for bias tape

1¼ yards fabric for backing

⅜ yard fabric for binding

Batting: 41″ × 41″

Thread to match the bias tape fabrics

Bias makers: ⅜″, ½″

Freezer paper

Mechanical pencil

Walking foot

◉ THE PATTERN

Using a compass, draw circles on plain paper or directly onto freezer paper with the following diameters:

2½″, 2¾″, 3¼″, 3¾″, 4″, 4⅝″, 5″, 5½″, 6″, 6⅝″

> For this quilt, piece the background first, then arrange circles over the top. Read through all of the directions first to get the big picture *before* you start. Susan finished the quilt top before quilting, but you could quilt the background *first*, then attach the circles. See pages 24 and 34 for more information about this quilting option.

◉ MAKE THE TEMPLATES

1. Trace each whole circle onto freezer paper. (Skip this step if you drew your pattern directly onto the freezer paper.)

2. Cut out the freezer-paper templates along the lines.

Whole-circle templates

◉ CUT OUT AND PREPARE THE FABRICS

1. From fabric #1, cut the following background pieces:

4 rectangles, each 8½″ × 16½″

4 squares, each 7¼″ × 7¼″

1 square, 14⅛″ × 14⅛″

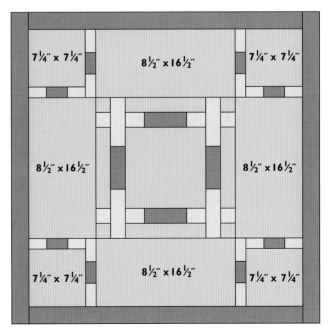

Background diagram (without circles)

2. From fabric #3, cut 4 strips, 2½″ wide across the width of the fabric.

3. From fabric #2, cut 2 rectangles, each 3¾″ × 16″. From fabric #3, cut 1 rectangle, 3½″ × 16″. Sew these 3 pieces together along the 16″ edges, with fabric #3 in the middle. Press the seams open.

4. Cut 8 pieces 1¾″ wide from the strip-pieced unit. Cut parallel to the *short* side, to make strips 1¾″ × 10″.

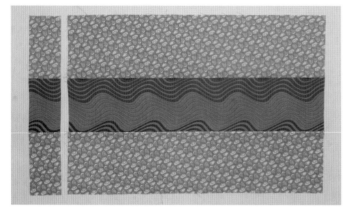

Cut 8 strips 1¾″ × 10″.

5. From fabric #2, cut 2 rectangles, each 7¼″ × 11″. From fabric #3, cut 1 rectangle, 5″ × 11″. Sew these 3 pieces together along the 11″ edges, with fabric #3 in the middle. Press the seams open.

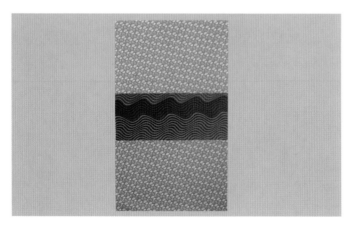

Strip-pieced unit

6. Cut 4 pieces 2¼″ wide from the strip-pieced unit. Cut parallel to the *long* side, to make strips 2¼″ × 18½″.

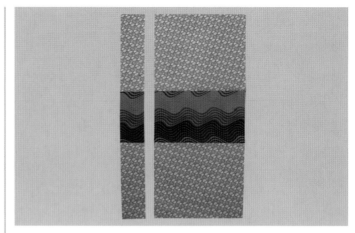

Cut 4 strips 2¼″ × 18½″.

7. Using the circle templates, cut the fabric circles. Start with 10 each of the 2½″ and 2¾″ circles, 5 of the 3¼″ circle, and 3 each of the remaining sizes. Place the waxy side of the template down on the right side of the fabric, and press. Cut out the circle shapes along the edge of the template (do not add ⅛″). Carefully remove the freezer paper; bend the paper a bit so it will release easily from the edges of the fabric.

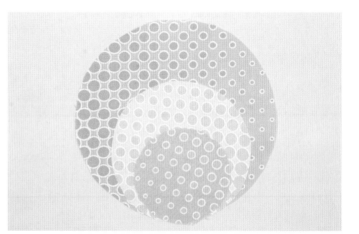

Cut circles from fabric.

Susan cut out a few circles from pieced Four-Patch blocks. To do this, sew 4 cut squares together. The finished block should be at least ½″ larger than the circle. Center the circle template over the square, and lightly press in place. Cut out the shape. This is an easy way to add more texture and movement to the quilt.

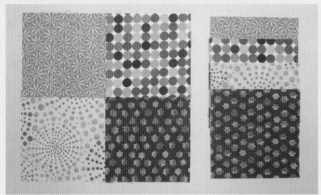

Four-Patch

Center template, and press.

Cut out pieced circle.

◎ CONSTRUCT THE BACKGROUND UNITS

CENTER SQUARE

1. Cut the large 14⅛″ × 14⅛″ square into 3 vertical pieces, beginning on the left side: 2¼″, 9½″, and 2¼″. Keep the order of the pieces intact.

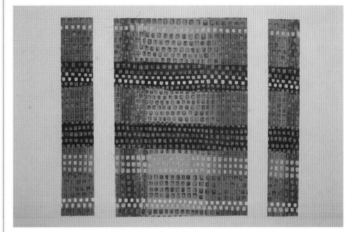

Keep pieces in order.

2. Insert 2 of the 2¼″ × 18½″ sashing strips (cut in Step 4 above) between the 3 pieces. Adjust the placement of the sashing so that the contrasting fabrics in each strip *do not* line up across the block. Sew the pieces right sides together. Press the seams open.

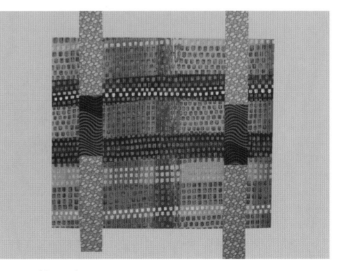

Insert sashing strips.

3. Cut the center square into 3 vertical pieces again, at right angles to the previous sashing inserts: 2¼″, 9½″, and 2¼″. Keep the order of the pieces intact.

Cut center square again, keeping pieces in order.

4. Insert the remaining 2¼″ × 18½″ sashing strips between the 3 pieces. Adjust the placement of the sashing as in Step 2, so that the contrasting fabrics do not line up. Sew the pieces right sides together. Press the seams open. Trim the ends of the sashing strips, squaring the unit to 16½″ × 16½″.

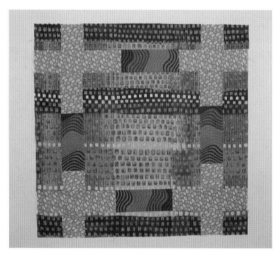

Finished center square

CORNER SQUARES

1. Place the 1¾″-wide sashing strips along 2 adjacent sides of 1 small square. Adjust the strips so the contrast fabrics are not centered or symmetrical.

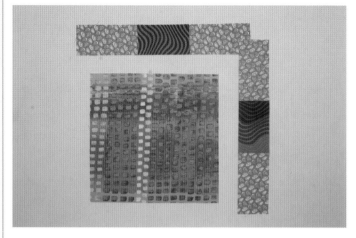

Sashing strips intentionally offset

2. Place 1 sashing strip right sides together with the square, and sew together. Press the seam open. Trim the ends. Repeat with the second sashing strip.

Finished corner square

3. Repeat Steps 1 and 2 to make a total of 4 corner squares.

◉ ASSEMBLE THE BACKGROUND

1. Lay out the pieced units and the rectangles to form the background.

Lay out units.

2. Sew the units together into rows. Sew the rows together. Press the seams open.

3. Pin the fabric #3 border pieces to 2 opposite sides of the background, and sew using a walking foot. Trim the border strips even with the quilt top. Repeat for the remaining 2 sides.

Finished background with border

 **tip** You can stack up to 3 circles on top of each other or overlap them, as Susan did. To cover the curves of stacked circles, start with the inner circle first and work out toward the outer circle. For overlapped circles, cover the curves of the circles underneath first, and then top with the overlapped circle. Choose fabrics that won't allow the print underneath to show through, unless that is the look you want.

Evenly stacked circles

Offset stacked circles

Overlapped circles

◎ LAY OUT THE CIRCLES

1. Use the photograph of the quilt as a guide for the placement of your circles without trying to duplicate the placement exactly. Let your fabrics speak and tell you where they want to go. Use fewer circles, or make more as needed. When you are satisfied with the arrangement, pin each circle in place.

2. Zigzag the raw-edge curve of each circle using a walking foot. Use a narrow but open zigzag. Stay right on the edge of the fabric, lifting the presser foot and pivoting as needed. Remember, the bias tape will cover up any uneven stitching.

tip

Susan read the directions about zigzagging the raw edges of the curves, but she skipped the step: she didn't think it applied to her. While quilting, she noticed raw edges pulling out from under the narrow bias tape. Fortunately, she was able to repair them and carry on. Sometimes we can successfully modify instructions, but in this case, zigzagging is an important and necessary step. Now Susan says, "Zigzag every time!"

◎ MAKE THE BIAS STRIPS

Review pages 14–17 for making and storing bias tape.

1. Make a batch of $3/8$″ and $1/2$″ bias tape from your chosen fabrics. Cut 12 strips $3/4$″ wide and 12 strips 1″ wide. Make more bias tape later if needed.

2. Wrap the bias tape around a piece of cardboard, and pin until you are ready to use it.

◎ COVER THE CURVES

Review pages 18–21 for making continuous loops of bias tape. The measurements provided here work with the circle template sizes for this project.

1. Use the measurements in the following chart to arrive at the cut lengths needed to make the bias tape. For other circle sizes, add $3/4$″ to the circumference length for $3/8$″ bias tape, and add 1″ to the circumference length for $1/2$″ bias tape.

Circle Template Diameter	Finished ⅜″ Bias Length to Cut ¾″ Bias Strips	Finished ½″ Bias Length to Cut 1″ Bias Strips
2½″	8⅝″	8⅞″
2¾″	9½″	9¾″
3¼″	11″	11¼″
3¾″	12⅝″	12⅞″
4″	13⅜″	13⅝″
4⅝″	15⅜″	15⅝″
5″	16½″	16¾″
5½″	18⅛″	18⅜″
6″	19⅝″	19⅞″
6⅝″	21⅝″	21⅞″

2. Join the cut ends right sides together, lining up the sides. Mark, and then stitch the diagonal seam. Trim the excess fabric, leaving a $1/4$″ seam allowance. Press the seam open, and then refold the bias tape.

Join ends right sides together with diagonal seam.

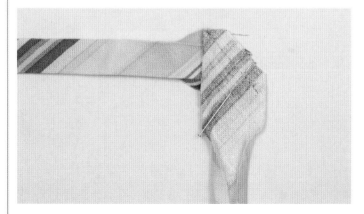

Stitch seam; trim.

3. Fold the loop of bias tape to mark the quarter points with pins. Fold the freezer-paper template into fourths. Use the fold lines to mark the quarter points on each fabric circle.

Find quarter points on bias tape and fabric circle.

4. Pin the bias tape loop to the circle of fabric, matching up the pins on both. Ease in the bias tape between the pins, using 1 or 2 additional pins in each quarter. Adjust as needed to make the bias tape round and smooth looking. Mist with water, and lightly press to bend the bias tape into the curve.

Pin, mist, and press.

5. Stitch the bias tape loop in place, starting with the inner circle first, using a walking foot, and removing pins as you sew. Don't backstitch; instead leave a thread tail and pull the top thread through to the back and tie off after stitching around the circle. Repeat for each circle.

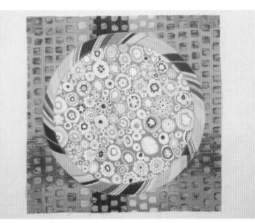

Finished loop

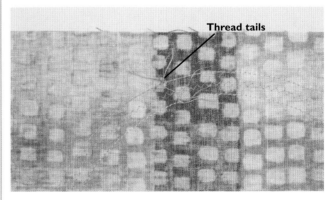

Thread tails

Tie off on back.

◎ FINISH THE QUILT

Review pages 22–26 for more information about quilting, sleeves, binding, and labels.

1. Layer the quilt top with the batting and backing fabric, and secure. Quilt the layers together by hand or machine. Use a wavy-line grid pattern as Susan did, or use your own quilting ideas.

Wavy-line grid quilting

2. Add a sleeve along the top edge for hanging the quilt. Bind the edges using your favorite method. Please add a label to the back of your quilt for family, friends, and quilters today and for curious quilt lovers and historians in the future.

But Wait, There's More

It's amazing how many times we can look through a collection of block patterns and notice new patterns each time. Make a cup of tea, and browse through your favorite encyclopedia, keeping a lookout for patterns with whole circles. Although it was difficult to pick just four, here are my current favorites.

◎ SAWTOOTH STARS

This is my variation of a traditional block known by many names, including Moon and Stars. My setting uses 2 different sawtooth star blocks. The first is a double sawtooth star, one inside the other. The second block combines the small

sawtooth star and circle unit with checkerboards. Alternated in the layout, they make a diagonal checkerboard chain.

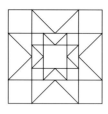 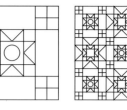

Sawtooth star blocks

◎ PIECED BLOCK WITH WHOLE CIRCLE

There are many variations of traditional patterns similar to this. With bias-covered curves, these blocks are not hard: piece the square first, place a circle over the square, and bias cover the curves. Carry on to finish the pattern with or without sashing.

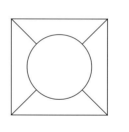 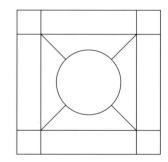

Block variations

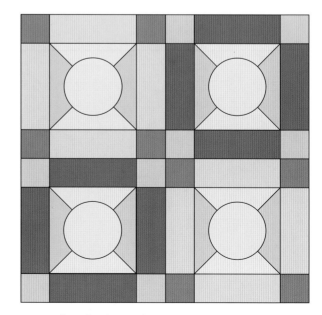

Pieced sashing makes jazzy secondary pattern.

◉ PIECED RING

If you've ever been tempted by this kind of block, but didn't want to deal with appliquéing the whole circle, now is your chance. Foundation piece the ring of points. Place the ring on a background fabric, or build the block with a center circle, the pieced ring, and the background on a foundation material, such as Sulky Soft 'n Sheer. Cover the curves, lining up the edge of the bias tape with the points on the pieced ring. It's as easy as that—honest!

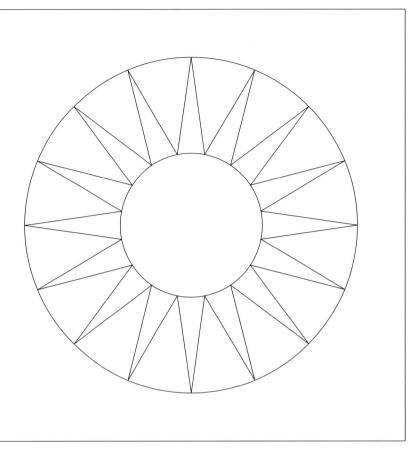

Pieced ring block

◉ LADYBUG BLOCK

Pieced or appliquéd bugs, animals, letters of the alphabet, and more have a long history in quiltmaking. Here are two ladybug blocks. The first is a traditional block; the other is a variation by Karla J. Rogers. In her bright, whimsical quilt, Karla layered the ladybug shapes and then folded the bias back on itself to cover the wings and the points of the leaves.

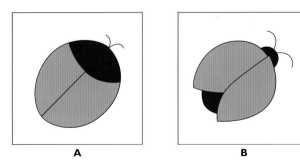

A   **B**

Ladybug blocks: Ladybug A is traditional block; Ladybug B designed by Karla J. Rogers.

The Well Watered Garden, Karla J. Rogers, 56³/₄″ × 70″

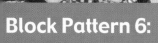

DOING WHEELIES

Spoked car rims inspired this floral fantasy. With the rim units clustered on a print fabric background, these circles look more like abstract flowers than car rims. Two borders, one narrow and one wide, give the quilt depth and grace.

TIVOLI GARDENS Wendy Hill, 39″ × 39″

Get to Know the Block

Just as the name "Doing Wheelies" implies, the inspiration for these blocks can be found in your driveway or a nearby parking lot. We are talking about car wheels—specifically the rim in the center of the tire. Once you start looking, you'll see quilt blocks in the rims of almost every car you see, but please let someone else do the driving while you go car rim sightseeing.

WHEELIN' AND DEALIN' challenge quilt, Joan Metzger, 48″ × 48″

Joan couldn't wait to take on the challenge of making a quilt based on car rims. After experimenting with different designs, she decided to make a sampler-type quilt with nine different car rim patterns. She used all three types: scoopers, spokers, and lattices. The dynamic background is assembled from bias cuts from one batik fabric. Other striped fabrics add accents. Extra batting behind the car rims gives the circles added dimension. Joan has lots more car rim quilt ideas—I wonder what she'll come up with next!

RIM RUNNER Wendy Hill, 54½″ × 21″

This sampler quilt shows off all three kinds of car rims: scoopers, spokers, and lattices. Use this quilt as a table runner or as a vertical or horizontal wallhanging, depending on the space. Frame each block with strips of various widths. Square up the new block, and finish assembling the quilt top with border strips.

SAMPLE BLOCKS

Check out these individual blocks for more ideas about how to change the look of car rim patterns with different fabric choices. Let car rims inspire your next quilt. Whether you make individual blocks or cluster the rims on a background, these blocks are a whole lot of fun to make. Remember to carry a camera with you in the car—just in case you see a dynamite car rim.

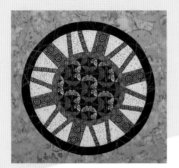

Spoker rim radiates warmth with these fabric choices.

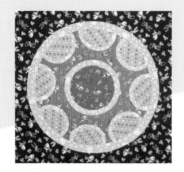

Western-themed fabrics make a cute scooper rim block.

Curved spoker rim pattern packs punch with these colors.

MAKE IT YOUR OWN

I've used three generic types of rims easily adapted for the bias-covered curve technique.

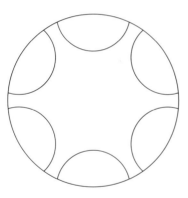

Scoopers—rims with cutout scoops

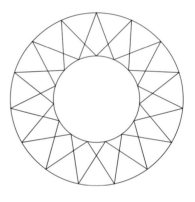

Lattices—rims with straight or scalloped patterns

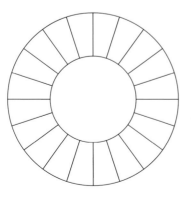

Spokers—rims with straight or curvy spokes

To make scoops, use partial circles or draw them freehand. Create the spokes with self-made bias tape. The spokes don't have to bend, so you can make these strips from fabric cut on the straight of the grain. Draw the lattice lines, and cover with bias tape; the following Get Started Project will rev you up.

After you have your patterns, use them in blocks or in clusters. Make a repeat block, or make a rim sampler quilt by mixing up different patterns. Personalize the rim patterns for the car lovers in your life, or use the rims as inspiration without telling anyone the design comes from a car wheel. Who knows where the possibilities will take you!

It's easy to trace around found kitchen objects to draw circles, or you can use a compass. By folding the paper circle over and over, you will have divisions of 4, 8, 16, or 32 without using a protractor. The divisions guide placement of the scoops, spokes, or lattice lines. For car rims with 3, 5, 7, 9, or other divisions, you'll need to use a protractor. Make templates for the components of the rim, and cover the curves with self-made bias tape. Just try one rim—and go from there.

Get Started Project

Review pages 7–13 for basic supplies and techniques.

Wheelie, Wendy Hill, 21½″ × 21½″; designed by Joan Metzger

◎ SUPPLY LIST

11½″ × 11½″ square lightweight fusible interfacing*

⅞ yard batik or woven stripe #1 for background**

½ yard stripe #2 for contrasting strip and corner triangles

⅜ yard fabric for large circle

⅜ yard fabric for ¼″ bias tape and small inner circle

⅜ yard fabric for ½″ and ¾″ bias tape

¾ yard fabric for backing

⅜ yard fabric for binding

Batting: 26″ × 26″

Thread to match bias tape fabrics

Thread to contrast with the large circle fabric

Bias makers: ¼″, ½″, ¾″

Marking pen or pencil

Permanent fine-point pen

Walking foot

*__Note:__ Use a lightweight fusible interfacing for this project to stabilize the center square when stitching the bias tape.

**__Note:__ Use the wrong side of half the rectangles to create the chevron pattern in the background. If you use a printed stripe, you will need an extra ½ yard of fabric.

◎ THE PATTERN

Use the pattern on page 92. You can trace it directly onto the fusible interfacing or onto freezer paper. Refer to Construct the Rim on page 87 for additional details.

> This quilt is constructed in two stages: the background and the rim. Quilt the background first, and then attach the rim. That makes it easy to quilt an overall pattern across the background, without having to stop and start around the car rim.

tip Joan adapted the following method for her larger quilt, *Wheelin' and Dealin',* on page 81. She quilted each section of the top to the batting only. Then she attached the rims to each section, with extra batting and more quilting around the parts of the rim. She sewed the sections together, using a ³⁄₈″ seam allowance and pressed the seams open. Finally, she layered the finished quilt top with backing fabric and stitched in the ditch to connect all three layers together. This method of working with small sections at a time makes it easier to do more intricate quilting.

◉ CUT OUT THE FABRICS

1. Refer to the diagrams to cut your fabrics.

From Stripe #1, cut on the bias:

4 squares, 8″ × 8″

4 squares, 3½″ × 3½″

8 rectangles, 3½″ × 8″

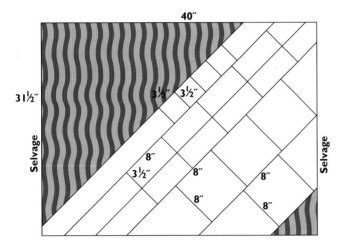

Cutting diagram for bias squares of Stripe #1

From Stripe #2, cut:

4 strips, 1″ × 13″ (cut so stripes are horizontal)

4 squares on the bias, 3½″ × 3½″

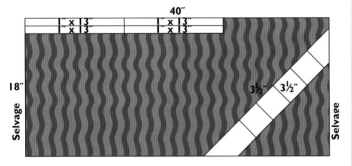

Cutting diagram for squares of Stripe #2

2. Make a freezer-paper template for the small center circle using the pattern on page 92. Place the template on the right side of the fabric, and press with a warm iron. Cut out the circle pattern piece and set aside for later. Do not add the extra ⅛″.

◉ CONSTRUCT THE BACKGROUND

Handle the bias-cut pieces with care. Be sure to place the iron and press—if you slide and glide the iron, the pieces will stretch.

CENTER SQUARE

1. Cut one 8″ square on the diagonal, cutting parallel to the stripes.

Cut in same direction as stripes.

2. Insert the 1″ strip of fabric. Center the triangles on each side of the strip, and stitch with a ¼″ seam allowance. Press the seam allowance toward the strip, and square up the corners. The square should measure 8″ × 8″.

Square with strip inserted

3. Use the following shortcut method to add a triangle to a corner of the square (a corner with contrasting fabric). Place a 3½″ contrasting striped square on the corner, right sides together, and line up the stripes in the square with the stripes in the background fabric. Draw a line from corner to corner, perpendicular to the stripes, and stitch along the line.

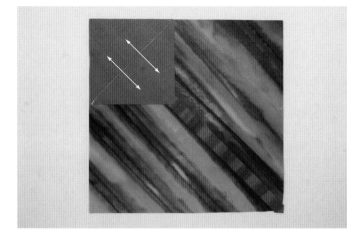

Make sure stripes run in same direction as background.

Trim off the excess, leaving a ¼″ seam allowance. Press the triangle toward the corner.

Trim excess.

Press carefully.

4. Repeat Steps 1–3 to make a total of 4 pieced squares.

5. Lay out the 4 squares so that the triangles are positioned on the outer 4 corners. Sew the squares together. Press all of the seams open. Since the intersection will be covered with the car rim, it doesn't matter if the seams don't match perfectly.

Finished center square

BORDER

1. Sew 2 rectangles together, positioned so that the stripes create a V, or chevron design, at the center seam. This is when you will need to flip 1 of the rectangles to the other side. Press the seam open. Repeat to make a total of 4 rectangle border units.

V at center seam

2. Use the following shortcut method to make 4 half-square triangle units. Place 1 each of the fabric #1 and #2 striped 3½″ squares right sides together, making sure the stripes of both are going in the same direction. Draw a line from corner to corner, going *across*, or perpendicular to, the stripes. Stitch along this line.

Stitch along marked line.

3. Trim off the excess on 1 side, leaving a ¼″ seam allowance. Discard the extra triangles, or save them for another project. Press the seam open.

Trim excess.

Finished half-square triangle

4. Repeat Steps 2 and 3 to make a total of 4 half-square triangle units.

5. You'll need the half-square triangles and 2 of the rectangle units to assemble 2 borders. Set aside the remaining 2 rectangle units for now. Position and sew a half-square triangle to each end of the rectangle units so the stripes create a V shape at the seamlines. Repeat to make 2 long border strips.

Stripes form V at seamline.

ASSEMBLE THE BACKGROUND

Lay out the background and border pieces for assembly. Sew the 2 short rectangle units to the center, right sides together, matching up the center seamlines. Press the seams open. Add the 2 border strips with corner units, matching up the seamlines. Press the seams open.

Arrange pieces. Sew together.

QUILT THE BACKGROUND

Layer the background with batting and backing fabric. Quilt a grid over the entire background, or use your own quilting designs. When finished, set aside the quilted background while you make the car rim.

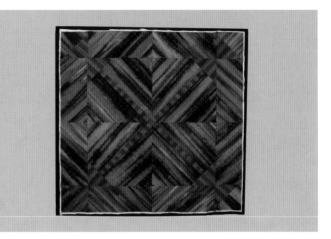

Quilted background

Note: If you prefer, you can skip this step and do the quilting after the quilt top is fully assembled.

MAKE THE BIAS TAPE

Review pages 14–17 for making and storing bias tape.

1. Cut 11 bias strips ½″ wide, and make a batch of ¼″ bias tape. Cut 1 bias strip 1″ wide to make a piece of ½″ bias tape. Cut 2 strips 1½″ wide, join the ends with a diagonal seam, baste the seam open, and make ¾″ bias tape.

Baste seam open.

2. Wrap the bias tape around a piece of cardboard, and pin until you are ready to use it.

⊚ CONSTRUCT THE RIM

See pages 17–21 for pinning, bending, and stitching continuous loops of bias tape.

1. With the smooth side up, center the square of lightweight fusible interfacing over the pattern. Tape in place. Trace the car rim pattern on page 92 onto the interfacing with a fine-point permanent pen. The glue bumps can make the line a bit wobbly—that is okay. See Tracing Option at right for an alternate method.

Trace pattern.

2. Place the square of interfacing *glue side down* on the *wrong* side of the fabric for the large circle. Fuse with a warm iron, following the directions with the product. Cut out the square along the edge of the interfacing.

3. Carefully sew along the marked lines, using a contrasting thread color. These stitched lines will be your magic guides for placing the bias tape on the right side of the fabric. I like this method of "marking" because you trace only once and then sew. If you prefer to trace the design onto the fabric, use the Tracing Option.

Stitch guidelines for bias tape placement.

TIP — TRACING OPTION

You can mark your background fabric with a fabric marker if you choose. You can use the pattern and simply trace the design onto your fabric, placing it on a lightbox if needed. You can also trace the design onto freezer paper and press the freezer paper to the wrong side of your background fabric and trace. Remove the freezer paper, and fuse the unmarked square of interfacing to the wrong side for stability when stitching the bias tape.

4. Cut the ¼" bias tape into 32 pieces, 5¼" long. Place, pin, press, and stitch the bias tape over the curves in one direction first. Make sure you don't stitch beyond the marked lines of the design. You'll need to trim off the excess bias tape. Then reverse directions and place, pin, press, and stitch the bias tape over the remaining curves.

Always stitch inner curves first.

5. Peel the freezer-paper template off the cutout small circle. Center and pin the small circle onto the large circle, using the stitched line as a guide. Zigzag around the outside edge of the small circle.

Zigzag around circle.

6. To make the continuous loop of bias tape for the inner circle, cut the $\frac{1}{2}''$ bias tape $11\frac{3}{4}''$ long. Place the ends right sides together, mark the diagonal seam, and stitch along the line.

Sew diagonal seam.

Trim the excess fabric, leaving a $\frac{1}{4}''$ seam allowance. Press the seam open, and refold the bias tape.

Finished loop of $\frac{1}{2}''$ bias tape

7. Fold the continuous bias tape loop to mark the quarter points with pins. Fold the freezer-paper template for the small circle into fourths. Use the fold lines to mark the quarter points on the small circle in the car rim.

Mark quarter points.

8. Pin the bias tape loop to the circle, matching up the pins on both. Ease in the bias tape between the pins, using 1 or 2 additional pins in each quarter. Adjust as needed to make the bias tape loop round and smooth looking. Mist with water, and lightly press to bend the bias tape into the curve.

Pin bias tape loop over circle.

9. Stitch the inner curve first, then the outer curve, using a walking foot and removing pins as you sew.

10. Cut out the finished car rim along the outer stitched line.

Cut out car rim.

1. Center the car rim on the quilt top. Pin. Zigzag the outer edges of the circle.

Zigzag raw edge of circle.

2. To make the continuous loop of ¾″ bias tape for the outer circle, cut the ¾″-wide bias tape 34½″ long. Follow the same process as Step 6 on page 88 (Construct the Rim): join the ends right sides together, mark the diagonal seamline, and stitch; trim the excess fabric, leaving a ¼″ seam allowance, press the seam open, and refold the bias tape.

3. Fold the continuous bias tape loop to mark the quarter points. Make a paper template for the large circle. Fold the paper circle into fourths. Use the folds on the template and pins to mark the quarter points on the car rim.

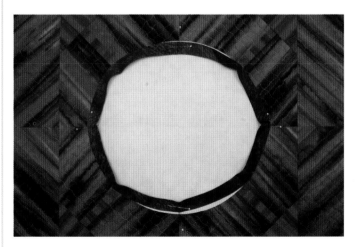

Mark quarter points on bias tape and car rim.

4. Pin the bias tape loop to the circle, matching up the pins on both. Ease in the bias tape between pins, using 1 or 2 additional pins in each quarter. Adjust as needed to make the bias tape loop round and smooth looking. Mist with water, and lightly press to bend the bias tape into the curve.

Use 8 to 16 pins to pin bias loop.

5. Stitch the inner curve of the bias tape first. Stitch the outer curve. Pull the thread ends to the back of the quilt. Insert the thread ends through a needle, tie a knot, and bury it in the batting.

FINISH THE QUILT

Review pages 22–26 for quilting, sleeves, binding, and labels.

If you didn't quilt the background already, now is the time to quilt. Use an overall quilting pattern that crosses over the car rim or a pattern that goes around the car rim.

For those who have already done the quilting, you may leave the quilt as is or add more quilting inside the car rim itself. For example, outline quilt the inner continuous loop of bias tape. If you are really ambitious, quilt around the narrow bias strips that make the curvy line pattern.

Add a sleeve along the top edge if you plan to hang the quilt. Bind the edges, using your favorite method. Please add a label to the back of your quilt for family, friends, and quilters today and for curious quilt lovers and historians in the future.

But Wait, There's More

Wheel patterns have a long history in quiltmaking. Variations include one wheel per block; others make wheels in the secondary pattern. I've chosen four of my favorite wheels for you to consider. Apply the same techniques presented in this book to adapt these wheel variations. Use freezer-paper templates, build the blocks on a foundation, zigzag the curves, and cover the curves with self-made bias tape.

WAGON WHEEL

I have always loved the wagon wheel block. Instead of piecing the spokes, use freezer-paper templates to cut out the spokes and zigzag them to the fabric circle. Cover the raw edges with bias tape. Then cover the curves, and you're done. Refer to the individual block photograph on page 82 to see how it works. It's so easy, I *will* have the time to make this quilt.

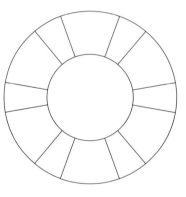

Wheel with 6 spokes

PROPELLER

This is an old block with many variations. I love the way women turned new inventions into quilt blocks, documenting our history through quilts.

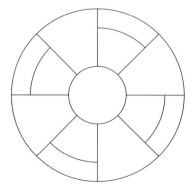

Interpret this traditional block in new ways.

◎ INTERLOCKED RINGS

These types of patterns make whole circles when the blocks are put side by side. They go by many names, including Royal Cross and Sunshine and Shadow. Instead of covering the curves on individual blocks, assemble the quilt top and cover the curves with continuous loops.

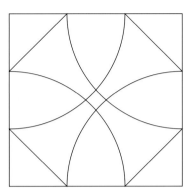

Interlocked Rings block

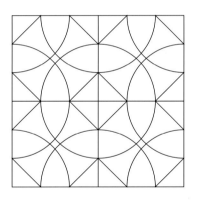

Secondary pattern emerges.

◎ CRAZY BULL'S-EYE

I adapted this pattern from a ceramic tile. I altered the pattern so that the 2 inner arcs will line up when placed next to other blocks; the other 2 arcs crisscross. I like the feeling of chaos and order at the same time.

Crazy Bull's-Eye block

RAZZLE DAZZLE Wendy Hill, 20½″ x 20½″

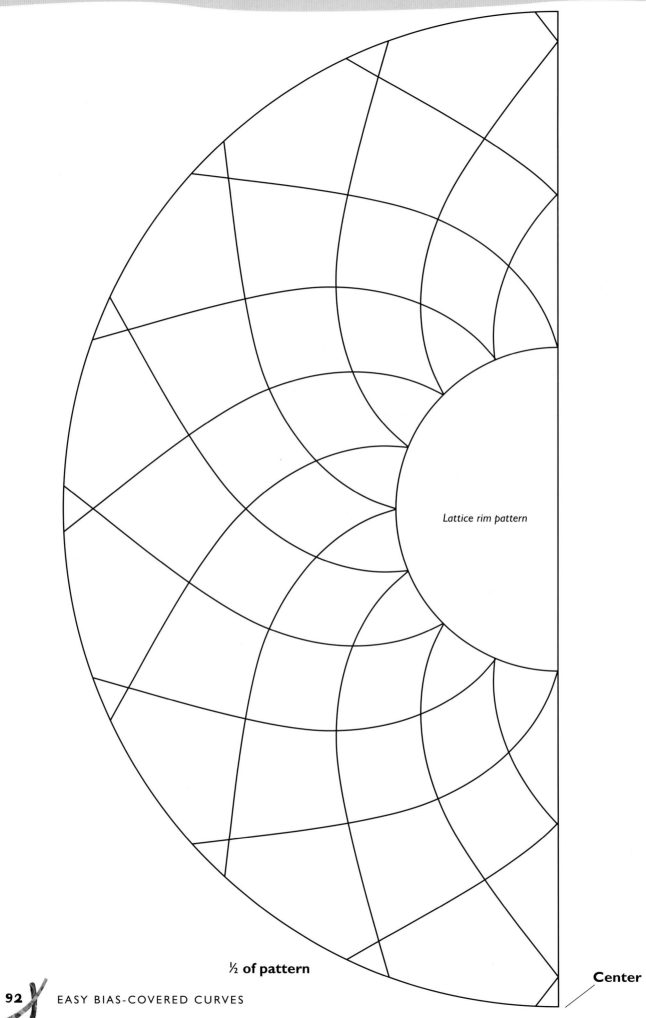

Lattice rim pattern

½ of pattern

Center

RESOURCES

Books

5,500 Quilt Block Designs, by Maggie Malone, 2003, Sterling Publishing Company, Inc., New York

All About Quilting from A to Z, from *Quilter's Newsletter Magazine*, *Quiltmaker*, and C&T Publishing, 2002, C&T Publishing, Concord, CA

Encyclopedia of Pieced Quilt Patterns, compiled by Barbara Brackman, 1993, American Quilter's Society, Paducah, KY

Q Is for Quilt, by Diana McClun and Laura Nownes, 2002, C&T Publishing, Concord, CA

Start Quilting With Alex Anderson, 2nd ed., by Alex Anderson, 2001, C&T Publishing, Concord, CA

Services

High Desert Custom Machine Quilting
Linda Bussey
La Pine, Oregon
541-536-1548
HiDesertquilting@direcway.com
See pages 5, 58, 59 and 66 for pieces quilted by Linda.

Quilting by Lori Gailey
Custom Quilting and Design Studio
PO Box 1136
Sisters, Oregon
541-549-6217
See page 39 for work quilted by Lori.

Studio Craig
Preserving quilts and other arts through photography.
Craig Howell
Phone: 541-388-5644
Fax: 541-318-5121
email: craig@studiocraig.com
website: www.studiocraig.com

Products

Quilter's Dream Batting
You can find Quilter's Dream Batting at your local quilt shops, or call: 1-888-268-8664 to find a quilt shop in your area. For more information about Quilter's Dream Batting, visit their website: www.quiltersdreambatting.com.

Sulky of America
Sulky provides a wide range of threads and stabilizers (water solubles, tear-aways, cutaways, and more), books, and other products, such as Sulky KK 2000, a temporary spray basting adhesive. For product information and retail and online sources, visit the company's website: www.sulky.com.

Timeless Treasures
For 100% cotton designs for quilting, craft, and apparel. Browse the collections on-line or find a retailer near you at Timeless Treasures' website: www.ttfabrics.com.

For More Information

Ask for a free catalog:
C&T Publishing, Inc.
PO Box 1456
Lafayette, CA 94549
800-284-1114
email: ctinfo@ctpub.com
website: www.ctpub.com

Quilting Supplies

Cotton Patch Mail Order
3404 Hall Lane
Dept. CTB
Lafayette, CA 94549
800-835-4418; 925-283-7883
email: quiltusa@yahoo.com
website: www.quiltusa.com

Note: Fabrics used in the quilts shown may not be currently available; fabric manufacturers keep most fabrics in print for only a short time.

Meet the Contributors

Detail of *Cool, Clear Water*, see page 29

JANE CROLEY

With her three older boys already in school, Jane thought she would have loads of time to make a king-size quilt when her daughter started kindergarten. That turned into one of the many learning experiences Jane had as she continued quilting through the years. When Jane met Wendy, she started seeing colors, shapes, patterns, and dimensions she never realized existed. Having Wendy as a mentor has been one of the treats of her life. Jane describes going from idea to finished quilt with *Cool, Clear Water* as a triumph in her life.

Detail of *Around and Around We Go*, see page 69

SUSAN HOWELL

Susan keeps busy with her work as Chief Operating Officer for Ralston360, a regional advertising agency, but she fills her spare time with quilting and enjoying the outdoors (climbing, hiking, skiing) with husband Craig. Susan's grandmother was an excellent seamstress and cook. A cousin inherited the cooking genes, which is fine with Susan because she inherited the sewing genes. Susan started her sewing with a required A-line skirt in home economics. But that didn't stop her from continuing to sew and eventually making quilts. Susan can't wait to retire so she can sew full-time!

Detail of *Whimsy*, see page 39

SUE MCMAHAN

Sue started making quilts in 1992. She rapidly became intrigued with antique quilts and the women who made them. Sue expanded her knowledge through a comprehensive long-distance course on the history of quilts, taught by Patricia Cox Crews of the University of Nebraska at Lincoln. Sue's growing interest in antique quilts led to interpreting traditional patterns with contemporary fabrics, particularly those with an Asian theme. Her studio has an inspiring view of the northern Cascade mountain range in Bend, Oregon, where she is a quiltmaker, teacher, and lecturer at venues such as Quilters Affair in Sisters, Oregon, and The Vermont Quilt Festival.

Detail of *Wheelin' and Dealin'*, see page 81

JOAN METZGER

In just the few short years since Joan began quilting in 1997, she has actively participated in and volunteered with her local quilt guild while showering her family with quilts of all sizes and styles. Recently Joan began entering her quilts in juried shows with great success. Joan is always ready to try something new, such as bias-covered curves!

Detail of *The Well Watered Garden*, see page 79

KARLA J. ROGERS

In the fiber arts, Karla found a wonderful outlet for her love of design, color, and textiles. She began sewing her own clothes at age ten and has had a passion for collecting, as well as making, quilts since the early 1970s. Currently a full-time wife, mother, and homemaker, she resides on a small farm in Nevada City, California, with her husband, son, and numerous members of the animal kingdom.

Detail of *AKA NO IN-EI (Shades of Red)*, see page 59

KATHY H. SHAKER

Kathy has enjoyed sewing and needlework since childhood. In middle school she earned the Betty Crocker Homemaker of the Year award! After a career in the high-tech industry, she retired to central Oregon, where she is an active member of her local quilt guild. She particularly enjoys playing with color and using embellishment to jazz up her quilts, and she firmly believes that one can never have too much fabric or too many beads. Kathy lives with her husband and three beloved cats.

Detail of *Whirlygigs*, see page 51

CAROL LOEHNDORF-WEBB

Carol's grandmother, a quilter, taught her to piece by hand when she was a pre-schooler. After a lifetime of designing and making clothing, Carol began to make quilts in earnest in 1986. Since then her quilts have been included in books and magazines and exhibited in national shows (with some bringing home awards). An honored Master Quilter in the Mountain Meadow Quilt Guild in Sunriver, Oregon, and a featured quilter in the Sisters Quilt Show in 2001, Carol brings a wealth of experience to her workshops.

Quilt Block Challenge Contributors

The people listed below took on the challenge of creating one or more blocks for the two challenge quilts. One person in each group wins the quilt!

Scrappy Circles Block Challenge

Detail of *Anything Goes*, see page 5

Judi Brown, Christine Hindle Drumright, Pauly Ruth Edwards, Sheila Finzer, Janet Gehlert, Susan Howell, Sarah Kaufman, Beverly King, Crys Kyle, Joan Metzger, Janice Mottau, Dolores Petty, Karla J. Rogers, Linda Saukkonen, BJ Tinker

30s Reproduction Fabric Challenge

Detail of *Friendship Ring*, see page 66

Carol J. Born, Diana Bos, Judi Brown, Christine Hindle Drumright, Carole Elsbree, Janet Gehlert, Susan Howell, Sarah Kaufman, Beverly King, Mary Klein, Joan Metzger, Karla J. Rogers, Linda Saukkonen, Kathy H. Shaker

MEET THE AUTHOR

Wendy remembers dreaming of colors when she was very young. Her first sewing projects were doll quilts and clothing. In high school, Wendy created a vinyl bikini bathing suit and a waterproof raincoat using bread wrappers. When her sewing teacher insisted it couldn't be done, Wendy made a faux fur coat with perfect bound buttonholes to prove that it could. More than 30 years ago, Wendy made her first big quilt: a replica of the floor of the Taj Mahal, in corduroy, for a king-size bed. The quilt covered the bed and extended to the floor. Creative work with fabrics and fibers, by both hand and machine, has been a steady force in Wendy's life.

Wendy's work has been in print in some form since 1992. She has contributed projects to several books and written magazine articles and three previous books (*On the Surface, Thread Embellishment & Fabric Manipulation* (1997), *Two-for-One Foundation Piecing, Reversible Quilts and More* (2001), and *Incredible Thread-A-Bowls* (2005) with C&T Publishing). Wendy follows her ideas wherever they may take her, from a reversible chicken/egg doll (Housewife Hen/Rietta on the Town) to thread-web quilts to bed quilts and more.

Wendy currently lives in Sunriver, Oregon, surrounded by bitterbrush, lava rock, a small grove of aspen trees, flocks of birds, and her family and friends. She travels extensively—to and from the grocery store and elsewhere on occasion. Her local quilt guild recently awarded her the title of Master Quilter, made all the more meaningful because it came from members of her community.

INDEX

Bias 14–21

Bias maker 16

Binding 25

Blocks 12–13

Borders 22

Clapper 7, 9–10

Fabric 8–9, 37

Pressing 9–10

Quilting 23–24, 34

Seam allowances 12

Soft 'n Sheer 7

Supplies 7

Templates 11

Topstitching 21

Zigzagging 13, 76

Quilts

A Little Whimsy 40

AKA NO IN-EI (Shades of Red) 59

Anything Goes 5, 35

Around and About 68

Around and Around We Go 69

Around and Around We Go Again 70

Butterfly Breeze 39

Circling the Block (detail) 6

Cool, Clear Water 29

Day and Night in the Garden 51

Drop in the Bucket 31

Fabricated Enigma 29

Friendship Ring 66

Girlie Girl 58

In the Woods 59

Razzle Dazzle 91

Really Red 60

Rim Runner 81

Rings 69

Roads Not Taken 28

Somewhere... 48

Tivoli Gardens 80

Tokyo Twist 38

Tutti Fruiti 50

Well Watered Garden, The 79

Wheelie 83

Wheelin' and Dealin' 81

Whimsy 39

Whirlygig 53

Whirlygigs 51

Windmills 56

Great Titles
from  C&T PUBLISHING

Foolproof curves
Quilts with Bias Strips & Continuous Paper Piecing
Barbara Barber

STRIPS 'n Curves
A New Spin on Strip Piecing
LOUISA L. SMITH

Pieced Curves So Simple
THE 6-MINUTE CIRCLE AND OTHER TIME-SAVING DELIGHTS
DALE FLEMING

CIRCLE PLAY
Simple Designs for Fabulous Fabrics
REYNOLA PAKUSICH

3-in-1 NEW & IMPROVED COLOR TOOL
NEW & IMPROVED
3-in-1 COLOR TOOL
NOW INCLUDES THESE MUST-HAVE TOOLS!
- *Numbered* Swatches
- *Two Value Finders* Green and Red
PLUS
- Color Guide
- Fabric Preview Windows

IDEAL FOR:
Quilting
Crafts
Home décor
Knitting
Sewing
Scrapbooking
Floral design
Graphic design!

JOEN WOLFROM

Color AND Composition FOR THE CREATIVE QUILTER
IMPROVE ANY QUILT WITH EASY-TO-FOLLOW LESSONS
KATIE PASQUINI MASOPUST AND BRETT BARKER